The Academic Community

DONALD E. HALL

The Academic Community

A Manual for Change

THE OHIO STATE UNIVERSITY PRESS
Columbus

Library of Congress Cataloguing-in-Publication Data
Hall, Donald E. (Donald Eugene), 1960–
    The academic community : a manual for change / Donald E. Hall.
    p. cm.
    Includes bibliographical references and index.
    ISBN-13: 978-0-8142-1062-8 (cloth : alk. paper)
    ISBN-10: 0-8142-1062-7 (cloth : alk. paper)
    ISBN-13: 978-0-8142-5161-4 (pbk. : alk. paper)
    ISBN-10: 0-8142-5161-7 (pbk. : alk. paper)
    [etc.]
    1. College teachers—Job satisfaction. 2. College teachers—Intellectual life.
    3. College teaching—Vocational guidance. 4. Learning and scholarship. I. Title.
    LB2331.H312 2007
    378.1'2—dc22
                        2007009708

This book is available in the following editions:
Cloth (ISBN 978-0-8142-1062-8)
Paper (ISBN 978-0-8142-5161-4)
CD-ROM (ISBN 978-0-8142-9138-2)

Cover and text design by Jennifer Shoffey Forsythe
Type set in Adobe Goudy
Printed by Thomson-Shore, Inc.

The paper used in this publication meets the mimimum requirement of the American
National Standard for Information Sciences—Permanence of Paper for Printed Library
Materials. ANSI Z39.48-1992

9 8 7 6 5 4 3 2 1

. . . .

Contents

. . . .

Acknowledgments

*t*HE MANY wonderful mentors and role models I have had in my
career to date have been too numerous to mention here. Let me just
say that I appreciate immensely the fine work that is being done both at
California State University, Northridge and at West Virginia University,
and I value highly the community of faculty, staff, students, and administrators at both institutions. I have learned much and continue to learn
daily from you all.

I want to thank the editors of InsideHigherEd.com (Scott Jaschik,
especially) who published a series of essays based on material in chapter 3 of this book and also the many online respondents to those essays
who provided me with excellent suggestions for revision and fine-tuning. I want to thank the editors of the journal *Pedagogy* who published
an excerpt from chapter 2 of this book and whose anonymous readers
provided much useful feedback. Gerald and Cathy Graff, thank you also
for the exchanges we have had on the topics raised in that excerpt and
chapter. And, finally, thank you to the audiences of talks I have given at
the University of Manitoba, the University of Malmö (Sweden), and the
Modern Language Association annual conferences who provided many
helpful suggestions and rejoinders to this work as it was in process.

Finally, I want to thank my partner, Bill Maruyama, for his support
and for his patience with the oddities and unpredictability of our shared
academic life. With much love, this book is for him.

introduction

. . . .

Academic Communities
from the Inside Out

i BEGIN HERE with a few autobiographical remarks, not because I think my life story is particularly remarkable, but rather because we all start from our own idiosyncratic positions and too often those are simply left unacknowledged or are assumed to be transparent. Of course, to foreground and denaturalize them is not the *best* we can do; it is, in fact, the *least* we can do if we are going to be responsible contributors to a conversation that involves and also greatly exceeds us. Despite media stereotypes of the absentminded or shy and fumbling professor, we who work in the academy are far from a homogeneous group. Indeed, our passions, career venues, and daily lives have a multiplicity that is often obscured even in our own work concerning our profession, work that too commonly reflects the perspectives of elite university faculty only. Our professional lives are narratives of sorts, and I have long believed that we need to hear about and learn from a far wider spectrum of those narratives. Only by placing narrative against narrative (against narrative against narrative), do we acquire some marginal ability to rewrite, synthesize, or even reject the stories that we have internalized or embraced as the singular truth about professorial life.

Having reached my mid-forties now, I've had a relatively successful career at two American institutions whose work I respect immensely. I have also lived and taught in Africa and Europe, held several administrative posts, and published nine books of various sorts. It has been a varied life involving volunteerism with an array of social service organizations, as well as teaching and writing, with good friends and colleagues, and a relationship with my partner stretching back many years now. I am lucky to be invited occasionally now to lecture abroad and to have professional and social ties across several continents. It is not a particularly unusual life, just a happy one with some lively national and international aspects.

But as I talk with colleagues about professional experiences I have had in Rwanda, Austria, or Finland as a department chair, gay rights activist, and modestly successful writer, the conversation sometimes turns to where I was born and raised, and at that point some of my conversation partners express surprise. I grew up in rural Alabama, went to a very small K-12 school, was the first in my direct family line to go to college, and did so over the objections of my father and despite the indifference of some teachers. There were some wonderful, positive influences that I encountered in Chelsea, Alabama, and at its high school, but also a sort of inertia there and in my extended family that meant that everyone else (almost, before me) got "stuck" (or, more generously, laid down roots) and is today still there, working in a trade (as my father wanted me to do), and living a conservative, religious life with boundaries stretching only as far as the county or state line.

I could write endlessly about why I was absolutely determined to get out of Alabama from a relatively early age. Television in the 1970s was a very big influence, as were movies. I had a few cousins who lived in far-away California, and when they came to visit, with their different accents and points of view, they certainly demonstrated that it was possible to leave and thrive. They and TV provided visual and aural proof of an "outside" to my immediate context, helped denaturalize it, and implied, at least, a position of critique that broadened my life-conversation and complicated those voices that were local and often quite self-satisfied.

However, the activity that performed the function of expansion and denaturalization more consistently than any other was reading. I've written before about the dynamic influence in late adolescence of my discovery of Walter Pater, Oscar Wilde, and existentialist philosophy, but years earlier (at age eleven or so) I found I could escape daily into the worlds of science-fiction novels. After I exhausted the meager library holdings available locally, I joined the "Science Fiction Book Club" at age thirteen and monthly in my rural mailbox appeared books that took me dramatically outside of my context of noisy chicken farms and rumbling coal trucks. Since I didn't have an allowance and had little way of earning money at that age, these were books that I could buy only by secretly selling to other students the school lunch tickets that my parents bought for me. But the difficulties involved were more than repaid in the hours spent with Isaac Asimov, Ursula K. LeGuin, Robert Heinlein, Samuel Delany, Frank Herbert, and countless others. Sci-Fi provided an imagined "outside" position (far outside, of course) to the dreary inside of rural Alabama and one that played a key role in creating who I have become as an adult. The half dozen years or so that I spent moving from the "inside" of Alabama life to the "outside" of extraterrestrial narratives, and from the "inside" of hours spent in those narratives to the "outside" of my bedroom, house, and community, allowed for shifting and disparate points of critique for all of the "inside" positions involved—novel played against novel, novel against rural Alabama, and television and films were also used to critique both. There were other ways of being and knowing than what I saw around me daily (my later encounters with Sartre, Gide, and Camus were set up well), and from early adolescence I was hell-bent on exploring those other ontologies and epistemologies to the extent that it was possible. (In another book, perhaps, I'll write a bit about what my chance encounter with a copy of Xaviera Hollander's *The Happy Hooker* at age fourteen allowed me in imagining a sexual "outside" to the homophobic "inside" of the Bible belt—Hollander may have saved my life given the high suicide rate of lonely, oppressed queer youth in the United States.)

I have spent a few paragraphs writing about this dynamic because it is central to what will follow. Those restless spirals of moving from inside out and from outside in provide the engine of personal, communal, and political change. The local, entrenched, and thoroughly naturalized can only be transformed through some vision of or encounter with an "outside," even if one returns inevitably to the "inside" of the immediate and mundane. This is a version of what is known as the "hermeneutic circle"—a movement from a circumscribed local positioning to a much broader, even if only imagined, "macro" position, and then back again. A similar dynamic of "inside/out" is key, also, to queer theory of the last two decades, with Diana Fuss's anthology using that term to point out the necessary redeployment of what is at hand to move toward a broader or different vision of the future, and using an imagined outside to what is at hand to challenge and change the self-satisfied and parochial. Indeed, my intellectual investment in this dynamic is why I have felt equally at home in my career to date writing about changes in Victorian cultural norms, changes in sexual culture today, changes in our pedagogies, and changes in our academic institutions or behaviors. That inside/out, outside/in dynamic, as complicated and compromised as it always is, is not only my scholarly passion, it is my life's passion.

One result of that intense and ongoing interest was *The Academic Self: An Owner's Manual*, which I wrote a couple of years ago, and which focused on the individual as the agent of, and object of, change. It was written to counter the rhetoric of victimization that sometimes pervades academic life, rhetoric that suggests that we as graduate students and junior and senior professors, are powerless in the face of broad institutional and professional forces. While there certainly are oppressive situations that demand critique and redress, my point was that unless we also explore the extent to which we are responsible for our own behaviors, attitudes, and life situations, we will often remain complicit with the very hierarchies and norms that oppress us. Change begins at home, in a sense; if we cannot denaturalize our attitudes about our work and professional values, then we will often remain victims and even self-victimizers. A book, a voice from the margins, or an encounter with a different lifestyle or point of view can help provide the fulcrum necessary for first personal and then broader professional change.

Indeed, we always live and work in communities: of family members, friends, neighbors, and colleagues in our departments and universities. We may shift our own attitudes supply and substantially, but unless we commit ourselves also to more than simply self-directed work, what ultimately have we accomplished? I couldn't muster the energy to teach a class, participate in a university committee, or attend a political function if I did not believe that our communities matter far more than our "selves" in their individual or isolated existences. Communal change does not happen quickly, neatly, or linearly, but it does happen all the time, and it is crucial that we continuously explore the extent to which we as individuals have an ability to contribute to contextual change that is thoughtful and in line with our intellectual and political commitments.

While I could focus on any number of larger or smaller communities here, my specific interest will be in those most common aggregates for our professional lives: our departments, colleges, and universities, where change often occurs in ways that we find particularly distressing or oppressive. Indeed, outside forces of change are often the most anxiety-producing of all: the force of imposed budgetary cuts or resource shifts, the effect of political mandates or trustee-level redefinitions, the changes in direction effected by a new university president or college dean. While it is obviously open to discussion whether or not all of these are fully "outside" forces (it depends on how we define "outside," of course), they certainly are ones that a department, let us say, can be on the receiving end of, and that can feel oppressive. How we respond, however, is always within our control, as upcoming chapters will explore.

That same community, the department, can also change through inside forces and factors. The retirement of a colleague, the hiring of a colleague in a new field or with a different point of view, the tenuring of one individual or the move into administration of another—all of these can result in dramatic changes within the microcosm of an academic unit. I was hired in 1991 into an English department that was dominated by a group of unhappy men (and a few unhappy women) who were antagonistic toward new theories and methodologies and who were scathing in their comments about the shifting demographics of our student population. Junior colleagues were often reduced to tears in department meetings by the vitriol and sarcasm of some of these angry senior professors. Then, the state offered a series of generous retirement packages and nearly a third of the department left within two years. The mood and rhetoric of the department began to shift significantly because the most cynical people simply went away. Previously unimaginable changes in curriculum and hiring priorities became possible because certain people were no longer in the room during department meetings. Who took the retirement deal was something that we untenured professors had no say in, just as we had no say in the "outside" decision to offer the retirement package itself. However, what some of us in the department did with the opportunity afforded by that new climate certainly was within our control.

There are, of course, innumerable professional situations where individuals or groups do have such agency, if they wish to claim it, and all of them reflect the "inside/outside" dynamic that I mentioned earlier. In fact, what made many of my senior colleagues so miserable was the fact that they had lost—and refused to reclaim—a productive engagement with the larger flow of intellectual and professional conversation outside of their own circle of angry friends. They were isolated from their profession, their students, and their community. Those closed, internally reinforcing circles of resentment and feelings of victimhood are quite the opposite of the expansive and intellectually adventurous circles of professional growth and change that much of this book will discuss. Healthy professional life depends upon an inside/outside dynamic of exploration and engagement with the extralocal with a return then to the local—refreshed, renewed, and reinvigorated. Those excursions can occur at conferences, through reading about a changing discipline or profession, and even in energetic hallway conversations with colleagues.

Yet the possibility of productive change within a department also depends on the inside/outside dynamic of individuals making connections with constituencies and administrators from across campus, and using those outside connections to effect positive changes in their immediate communities. My department changed dramatically because over the course of the next ten years, some of us helped lead it in making over twenty tenure-track hires. We were often given those hires precisely because a few colleagues and I were very adept at talking with deans and university-level administrators; had proven that we would use resources wisely; and had negotiated over how best to reflect the changing priorities of the university, as well as our own interests and commitments. The best colleagues, administrators, and political activists whom I have known have always understood that inside/outside dynamic. Our professional lives are never lived in isolation, and our microcommunities are always only subsets of much larger groups, whose needs and perspectives must be explored and engaged if we are going to maximize our agency and exercise it in responsible ways.

If agency of a sort is almost always possible through those inside/outside dynamics (of consciousness and active engagement), then why, one might ask, do so few individuals and aggregates of individuals work to rethink their professional values and remake their institutions? Change is uncomfortable and nerve-wracking for anyone, but for academics, alone or in groups, embracing change means giving up one of the foundational myths of academic identity: the myth of mastery. To embrace change is to admit the imperfection of previous ways of being and conducting oneself, and even outright error or misunderstanding. To seek change is to admit humbly that one's current existence and one's current set of narratives are outdated or inadequate. To embrace the inside/outside dynamic is to admit the local, limited, and idiosyncratic nature of one's personal vision and set of answers to complicated questions. For the trained expert, hubristic intellectual, and masterful researcher and teacher, that admission can threaten a core component of a professional, and sometimes personal, life. In fact, for anyone clinging tenaciously to that myth of mastery and self-sufficiency, this book probably will have little value.

My belief is that most of us in the academy—skilled researchers, critical readers of texts, sensitive teachers, and caring colleagues—do not cling with desperate tenacity to our own authority and professional patterns. Oftentimes, we are simply invested in narratives and customs that we have yet to fully interrogate. Indeed, *The Academic Community: A Manual for Change* suggests that even the most tradition-bound and dysfunctional groups have the opportunity to redirect and reinvigorate themselves. Like *The Academic Self*, this book focuses on the individual as the agent of change, though here with an emphasis on working in and with a community of fellow teachers and scholars. Yet even if coalition-building and conversational processes must move well beyond the perspectives and input of the isolated individual, the responsibility for change always begins at the level of the individual professor or administrator. To put it bluntly: no one has more responsibility than you do for making your department, college, or university a better place in which to teach, conduct research, and live a multifaceted professional life. Others—deans, provosts, or presidents—may be paid far more than you are, and may even be explicitly assigned that task of improvement, but if you don't like certain aspects of your institutional environment, then it is your responsibility to try to do something about it, albeit carefully, responsibly, and in self-protective fashion.

Redirecting my focus for the present project from the "self" as the venue for change to the "community" as its venue means I must shift also some of my theoretical touchstones. *The Academic Self* referenced the work of the sociologist Anthony Giddens, who, in several works from the 1990s, explored today's unparalleled rhetoric of and potential for self-reflexive work. Giddens usefully, if perhaps overoptimistically, suggests that we late-modern individuals have given up our traditional narratives—of gender, sexuality, race, and class—and have therefore the potential for remaking ourselves at will and even from the ground up. While Giddens greatly underestimates the force of fundamentalist religious beliefs, the entrenched nature of gender definitions, and (perhaps most glaringly) the different capacities of people from various material circumstances and class backgrounds to *afford* the luxury of self-refashioning, he nevertheless highlights the potential that does often exist but that also often gets lost in our equally powerful fascination with victimization and blame placing. As I will suggest throughout this book, it is important to hear utopian voices (and I do consider Giddens utopian), use them as motivational devices and interlocutors with our own senses of limitation and sometimes helplessness, and think of them as one tool among many for effecting the changes that we desire.

And it is that emphasis on interplay and multiple voices that brings me to my theoretical touchstone for *The Academic Community*. I want to spend a few paragraphs here with Hans-Georg Gadamer, the originator of the field of philosophical hermeneutics, and with his notion of dialogue and critical agency. Gadamer, a German academic whose life spanned the twentieth century (he was born in 1900 and died in 2002), has been greatly underutilized to date in cultural studies, and completely ignored in professional studies. Part of this, as Kathleen Wright argues in an essay included in a recent volume of feminist interpretations of Gadamer, is attributable to the fact that his magnum opus, *Truth and Method*, was published in 1960 but first translated into English in 1975, and was "eclipsed right from the start by the intensity of the discussion about the works of Michel Foucault and Jacques Derrida" (Wright 2003, 40). Yet she and most of the other contributors to that volume argue that Gadamer's work is long overdue for an assessment by cultural critics because of his core belief in dialogue as the lived functional process by which we gain knowledge of ourselves, our limitations, and our necessary ties of respect and responsibility to others in our social and professional lives. Dialogue takes us outside of ourselves and allows us to return to those selves with a broader, altered vision. As I will explore in coming pages, a commitment to dialogue allows us to live a version of a hermeneutic circle.

In theorizing conversation as a way of life, Gadamer proposes that we must always put our "prejudices" or presuppositions at risk in seeking out others with whom to share ideas, test our notions of reality, and come, through an exchange of viewpoints, to some understanding of our own mistakes and misapprehensions. Risk taking, especially in this way risking our own core beliefs and sense of self-satisfaction, demands a certain conscious, even chosen, privileging of the communal over the selfish or self-serving. In a sense, Gadamer's then is an *ethics* of engagement with our colleagues, neighbors, and fellow inhabitants of the planet, for as Jean Grondin, his biographer, notes, "As Gadamer often says . . . 'The soul [of his philosophy] consists in recognizing that perhaps the other is right'" (*Philosophy of Gadamer*, 100) or as Gadamer himself states in *Truth and Method*, we must remain "fundamentally open to the possibility that the [other] is better informed than we are" (294). Indeed, Grondin isolates a key distinction in some of Gadamer's later work wherein the philosopher chastises those whom he calls "pedants" and distinguishes them from true intellectuals whom he values as "cultivated" for their nurtured and honed skepticism about the inviolability of their own opinions. In Gadamer's words, "The cultured person is the one who is ready to admit as plausible (literally, to value) the thoughts of others. . . . The cultured person is not the one who displays superior knowledge, but only the one who, to take an expression from Socrates, has not forgotten the knowledge of his ignorance" (quoted in Grondin 2003, 25). I am belaboring this point here a bit because Gadamer relates it explicitly to our work in the academy, in a profession devoted to developing "people's sense of judgment and ability to think for themselves" (Hoffman 2003, 103). As I will explore in a later chapter, Gadamer, in his own life as an academic, demonstrated how dialogue can contribute also to the process of community-building within a university setting.

Though Gadamer coined the term "philosophical hermeneutics," he drew on a long scholarly tradition. Hermeneutic theory, from early biblical scholars, to Friedrich Schleiermacher in the Romantic era, through Wilhelm Dilthey at the end of the nineteenth century, and up to and including Martin Heidegger, Paul Ricoeur, and Gadamer in the mid- to late twentieth century has as its common focus textuality, though with a variety of emphases. Gadamer's hermeneutics urges us to ask, how do we understand the written text, the textuality of phenomenon, and even the text of the self as conversant with the text of the world surrounding the self? Indeed, it is that emphasis on the self as text, always in a larger context, that allows a useful supplement to our understanding of how change occurs in our professional lives, because what Gadamer in particular does is emphasize the slowness of all change as it occurs within tradition and in negotiation with a variety of other conservative forces. Whereas Giddens posits us as free and posttraditional, Gadamer slows down our expectations even if he never denies the possibility of radical change over time.

The slowness of change can be explained by way of that concept mentioned earlier: the hermeneutic circle. Friedrich Schleiermacher, biblical scholar and the originator of modern hermeneutics, first theorized that we gain understanding of texts through an inside/outside movement, reading a passage in isolation and then placing it in the context of our knowledge or supposition concerning the whole, or larger, text. That continuous movement between the local, or micro, and the larger, or macro, is how we move responsibly through a text, and, in my argument here, how we move responsibly through a personal and professional life. Schleiermacher is rarely referenced today in literary studies because he urged the hermeneut to work toward an understanding of authorial intent, to place oneself in the position of the "originator" of the text. For Schleiermacher, "intent" was the ultimate and determining "macro." Indeed, this reverence for intent was adopted by a few archconservative literary critics of the twentieth century, such as E. D. Hirsch, who became known for their rejection of new methods and theories. However, phenomenologically based hermeneutic theory (coming from Heidegger, Gadamer, Ricoeur, and others) moved in a different direction, gave up completely any attempt to reconstruct "intent," and even found little value in those attempts, since we are always reading from our own position and belief systems. Even so, I argue that expressions of intent can themselves be textual. They should be part of what we respond to and work with as we engage in conversations with colleagues and administrators, with communities of students, and with the public. We can "read" intent as critically and productively as we can any other addition to a conversation.

Gadamer and hermeneutic theory offers professional studies some powerful tools. In foregrounding the hermeneutic circle, I will emphasize how our individual needs and desires as members of a community must always operate in negotiation with the macrolevel concerns of our departments and colleagues. Furthermore, our understanding of the dynamics of our department must always work in tandem with our explorations of the larger needs and priorities of our colleges and universities. And finally, our colleges and universities must operate responsibly with reference to and some understanding of the perspectives of their surrounding communities. That continuous movement from inside to outside and then back again propels responsible change at every level of professional engagement.

And this, Gadamer reminds us, happens most productively by way of a conversational process. We can only move from solipsism to responsible intellectualism by embracing our ties to others, and this means finding ways of engaging others in dialogue. Unlike the dynamic of reading a print text, when we are dealing with the text of our departments and universities, we have the opportunity to solicit responses, to ask for clarifications, and to explore more energetically an "outside" that may lead us to alter the "inside" of our own beliefs and localized interests. While I began this introduction with reflections on my own use of a sort of hermeneutic circle as an adolescent reading science fiction in my bedroom, the similarity with the work I am describing here is far from perfect, of course. Gadamer urges us to talk to others, to listen to them, to learn from their differing perspectives, and then to return to our "selves" with an altered vision. As an adolescent, I had primarily the words on the page (or emanating from the television) to use to alter my understanding. In the academy, we will make a grave mistake if we think we can "read" others' motives and perspectives from a distance, or if we read *only* memos, e-mails, or university documents and fail to engage the human beings behind the print. Textualization of the sort I am broadly discussing here, by way of hermeneutic theory, always carries with it the risk of objectification. Objectifying others is what we already tend to do too often; more of the same is not what I am calling for in this book.

Instead, what occurs in conversations that are eagerly joined and that flow from positions that are not self-satisfied is, in Gadamer's words, a "fusion of horizons." This is his concept for how differences—temporal, epistemological, cultural, and linguistic—meet and lead to change. It is the meeting of one worldview with another worldview, with those views shifting by way of the encounter. On the most mundane level, it is what happens when I read a novel about a place or person the likes of which or whom I have never encountered before. I see things differently through that encounter; my horizon of understanding shifts through a fusion with the horizon represented in the text. Cynically one could say that I simply find in the text whatever I need to confirm my own opinions or prejudices (Stanley Fish has made that argument repeatedly), but I believe otherwise. From interactions with students, friends, colleagues, and family, and from my experience of my own metamorphosing beliefs, I know well that people are not static and that their worldviews do change over time through a wide variety of encounters with texts, with people, and with new cultural contexts.

What Gadamer does emphasize, however, is that such change is usually incremental. Indeed, if we expect quick, radical change, we will often be disappointed. And I have a suspicion that it is from those overestimations of the pace of possible change that some cynicism in the academy derives. We can hope for, and even work strenuously for, fundamental—even radical—alterations in our institutions, our communities, and our global ways of being. However, if we expect to see quick results, we are fooling ourselves. As I argued over a decade ago in my first book on Victorian cultural metamorphosis, *Fixing Patriarchy*, change often occurs in ways that are visible only over the course of many decades and more. Gadamer slows down our expectations while never undermining our sense of long-term purpose.

In fact, some of my own purposes here warrant a bit more elaboration. While Schleiermacher would have us attempt to reconstruct authorial intent from afar, here you have an author willing to display his intentions, even if that transparency is never complete and unproblematic. Of course, my readers' perspectives on what I write will return to me in comments, e-mails, and reviews, and then feed back into my understanding of what I have done and would have done differently with the luxury of a broader vision. In the meantime, however, here is what I intend in the coming pages, and here are some of the specific agendas I am setting out for *The Academic Community: A Manual for Change*.

"Starting with the Self" examines how we conceive of our selves in the academy. The chapter looks at various figures from history and the academy who provide differing models for and enactments of intellectual and academic selfhood: George Eliot (whom I mentioned in *The Academic Self*), Friedrich Nietzsche (whose self-interested iconoclasm has greatly influenced current work in cultural studies), Paul Ricoeur and Angela Davis (as models of brave and supple teacher/scholars), and, finally, Gadamer (who lived a fulfilling and successful academic life, making positive contributions both to his home institutions and the field of philosophy). All of these figures (and the career models they provide) are discussed with the purpose of judging the effects and responsibility of their contributions to the conversations that surrounded them and that should concern us too.

"Creating Student Intellectuals" explores the community of the classroom and our responsibility as agents of change in our undergraduate students' lives. In the chapter, I engage in a dialogue with Gerald Graff's *Clueless in Academe* to discuss how we can best empower and educate our students to be responsible participants in their own conversations. I supplement Graff's perspectives with Gadamer's insistence on the necessary examination of "prejudice" as part of our training of, and work as, intellectuals, and complicate both with the Foucauldian emphasis on the specificity of successful intellectual work. All of these, I suggest, bear not only on what we do in the classroom as teachers, but also on the skill sets and passions that we attempt to nurture in our students for their use throughout their lives. Graff, working with Cathy Birkenstein, offers "templates" for encouraging students to argue their viewpoints; I offer instead prompts that get students to probe where those viewpoints come from.

"Changing Graduate Education" extends the previous discussion to address graduate education specifically. Here, I respond to a number of books already widely cited (including ones by David Damrosch and Bill Readings) to talk about some of the goals we might adopt for our graduate programs. I suggest that we move away from a model of training scholarly monologists, and move toward seeing graduate education as a venue where intellectual conversation is emphasized, and where academics-in-training learn to be community members. As members of intellectual communities, they certainly should learn to conduct research, but they must also learn collegial skills that allow them to participate in their departments, in their classrooms, and in the academic profession as a whole. If we move from the base assumption that we are training monologic scholars to a broader notion of training partners in conversation, we also dramatically broaden how that training effected. And even as we retain as an important goal helping graduate students get jobs in the academy, we do them an enormous service in training them for the wide variety of roles they will play as academics.

In "Building a Vibrant Department and University Community" I look at the transformational potential of a single department member or administrator who commits herself or himself to building a vibrant community. As in previous chapters, I focus on the energy and intellectual excitement of conversation. I examine the ways conversations can go awry in academic communities, but also how those conversations can be enhanced. The chapter emphasizes practical ways of energizing conversation: research workshops, roundtable presentations, faculty reading groups, and interdisciplinary speakers series and brown-bag discussions. I explore internal and external stressors that threaten departmental and institutional vibrancy and offer concrete examples of how the effects of these stressors can be mitigated.

"Reclaiming the University as a 'Public Good'" examines the general state of decline in the respect accorded public education in the United States. We have generally seen funding for state universities diminish to the point that formerly "state-funded" institutions are now only "state-assisted" ones. Indeed, education is no longer seen as a public good, only a private responsibility. I explore here ways of reconceiving the roles that universities play in their surrounding communities. They must add value to those communities and not only through vocational training. In fact, the conversations that I discussed in previous chapters should move beyond the physical boundaries of the campus. We must place greater value on public service by faculty members, commit ourselves to making publicly accessible the work that we do as academics, and create forums and venues to offer that work to the public. This demands also a renewed commitment to tenure and the protection of academic freedom, because such publicly visible work is always risky. However, as paid intellectuals (as I will argue throughout the book), such risk taking and broad public engagement should be considered an unquestionable core component of our vocational responsibilities.

The Academic Community concludes with an examination of how we might engage in the work I call for here but still protect our personal lives by setting sustainable goals and boundaries. The chapter discusses how we can arrive at a personal sense of "balance" in our academic lives and avoid bitterness and a sense of defeat. In understanding and accepting the incremental nature of change, even as we motivate ourselves with idealistic goals, we can maintain our commitments, retain our excitement about the conversations in which we participate, and continue to replenish our professional energy. Anything less than this necessarily complex and multilayered awareness is, in fact, unworthy of the intellectual talents we in the academy possess.

As I hope is apparent by now, this is a book animated by an optimism and sincere belief that our academic communities can be sites of transformation, in the lives of students, in our own professional self-conceptions, and in public intellectual life generally. While many of my examples in the coming pages are drawn from the humanities and arts, I hope this book, like *The Academic Self*, will find a much broader readership and contribute to exchanges in the social sciences, the healthcare fields, education departments, and the hard sciences. Similarly, this contribution is from the perspective of a full-time, tenured member of the academy, but I hope it proves useful as we think about how to improve the lives of part-timers, and those not on the tenure track. Our lives in our classrooms, department and professional meetings, and research venues (whether labs or offices) overlap and diverge in ways that I can only imperfectly imagine. This is my addition, from an inevitably and narrowly circumscribed perspective, to a highly dispersed and polyphonic conversation on what we do and who we are as academics. It is an interjection to which I hope to hear pointed and diverse rejoinders.

Indeed, the "academic community," as I am using the term here, should never be conceived of as a closed or inwardly focused system. The "ivory tower" exists only as a disabling myth. Our *communities* include overlapping and porously bordered conversational groups of two or three faculty members with similar research interests, students and faculty working in classrooms and on extracurricular projects, cross-disciplinary teams from different parts of campus, department and college administrators, trustees and others who demand accountability and respect for diverse beliefs, and finally the American and global communities in which we all must live our personal and professional lives. Each of these groups has needs and norms that are distinct but that can also overlap in ways that we have yet to fully acknowledge. If we retain our commitment to conversation as an ongoing process, one in which we participate as partners but not as determiners of outcomes, one that may reach temporary points of suspension but never a terminus or moment of triumph for one partici-pant, then we can minimize not only the risk of burnout but also of our own possible superfluity in contemporary American culture.

If "intellectual" and "academic" have become pejoratives, then we in the academic community must take responsibility for reclaiming them and reasserting their value and the value of the work we do. As effective communicators, supple thinkers, and well-trained teachers, we in the academy have all of the skill sets we need to serve as agents of change. The question remains: will *you* decide to do that hard work?

chapter one

Starting with the Self

$\mathcal{W}$ HILE LATER chapters of this book focus on the future of the many communities we participate in as teachers in the undergraduate classroom, as colleagues in departments and universities, and as mentors to graduate students and junior faculty, I first want to explore the academic selfhoods we currently enact, where they come from, and how we arrive at some ability to exercise agency (even if always imperfect and variously compromised) over them. For a few readers, I may linger in philosophical history here a bit longer than they might desire, but for most, I hope that the following discussion grounds this book (and, more important, professional studies as a field) in a rich preceding conversation on subjectivity and responsibility. In discussing the academic "self" and the academic "community" as dense and complex texts for which we are largely responsible, I suggest that this self- and community-directed work is as intellectually rich and ethically consequential as any other research or pedagogical project that might rivet our attention and engage our well-honed professional skills.

I have argued elsewhere that at least since René Descartes's early seventeenth-century formulation of his *Cogito* ("I think therefore I am"), and even more explicitly since John Locke's theorization of the "punctual self" half a century later, Western philosophy and social science have often implied a degree of instrumental (mechanical, and potentially even uninhibited) agency over selfhood (*Subjectivity*, 16–31). Discourses of religion, self-help, pop psychology, and advertising continue to encourage us to see ourselves as perfectible beings. Indeed, self-improvement can be a very laudable ideal. It does not have to involve cosmetic surgery, self-absorption, or tepid chicken soup for the soul; it can also motivate us to work toward any number of progressive social goals, including more humane and responsible ways of living in the world. However, such change does not come easily. Feminist, class, and race theorists, and others working out of identity political positions, have long explored how we, as acculturated beings, are not malleable pieces of clay, available for easy reworking. Our perspectives are formed through and rooted in language, ideology, tradition, and familial and extrafamilial experiences. Consciousness-raising is possible, to be sure, but becoming aware of the socially constructed nature of our selfhood only allows us a marginal ability to rethink and reshape it.

Nevertheless, the potential for a marginal degree of agency in self-directed change still carries with it considerable opportunity and responsibility. The Socratic comment that "the unexamined life is not worth living" rings true for many of us who self-define as intellectuals. It is equally the case that the unexamined life is often ethically irresponsible. This is most visible in national politics, where strident assertion has too often supplanted (and derided) earnest self-reflection. It can be evident at the personal and professional levels, where self-interest can too often go unchecked by a communal perspective. I would argue that we academics, in particular, have a fundamental responsibility to ask ourselves how our actions and interactions contribute positively or negatively to the realization of a more just and intellectually dynamic world, within our departments and more globally. As paid intellectuals, who have voluntarily (often aggressively) sought out and assumed an obligation for education and the creation of knowledge, I believe that the fulfillment of this ethical responsibility should be a core component of our professional self-definition (though certainly never mandated as an explicit component of our employment or tenure requirements—our work and worldviews are too diverse for that type of prescription and presumption).

Indeed, for the many academics who do desire to work toward more ethical and intellectually vibrant enactments of selfhood, a first step might be to ask where our professional selves actually come from. The answer will be as unique as the individual answering the question, but several possibilities spring to mind immediately. We learn how to *be* an academic through observing professors during our undergraduate years and graduate school training, through observing and modeling ourselves on friends and peers throughout our professional lives, and by reading about or listening to narratives concerning the career paths, choices, and priorities of other academics (such as those published in the "Careers" section of the *Chronicle of Higher Education*). In all of these instances, our professional models may be ones that we define ourselves largely through, in partial negotiation with, or even substantially against. Certainly, I have learned much about what not to do as a professor and administrator by observing the actions of a few colleagues whom I definitely do not want to emulate.

I could reference here Judith Butler's performance theory to talk about those roles that we enact and potentially alter as we perform them, but Butlerian theory does not deal directly with the textuality of phenomena, the ways that we literally "read" performance narratives at times, much as my own readers are now interacting with this page. As I suggested in my introduction, hermeneutics and Gadamerian theory, in particular, speak more directly to the topic of this book; it suggests that our selves are made up of narratives of sorts, and that we encounter (in a variety of formats) potential scripts or partial scripts that we can critique and customize as our own. Like all forms of "constructionist" theory, it emphasizes that there is no transcendental source of identity, wisdom, or priority for our life activities. All we have are the variety of roles, choices, articulations, and actions of others around us, and who have gone before us, and these are ones with which we must engage both critically and creatively.

In *The Academic Self* I asserted that we need more regular and dynamic occasions to share our professional life stories and styles so that the menu of choices that any of us can peruse increases and deepens in quickened conversation with our fellow academics. Yet certainly this same conversation can be held with predecessors and others, whose narratives, perspectives, and priorities we encounter only in written textual form. As I read, I always attempt to test my own life against what I am reading. Indeed, the narratives that I encounter, whether in aural, visual, or written format, are ones that I always work to bring into engagement with my own continuing life narrative. This engagement constitutes the phenomenological process of life itself for all of us, but the question remains, to what extent are we aware of it and able to exercise agency through it? It can (and should) provide ample occasions for conscious critical and intellectual work. If we in higher education, and especially those of us in the arts, humanities, social sciences, and education, are largely defined as professionals by the success of our interpretive abilities—and are trained especially in the skills necessary for careful and multilayered responses to written texts and data—then we should be well-poised to engage thoughtfully with narratives of professional success and failure, functionality and dysfunction. As hermeneutic theorist Paul Ricoeur notes, our task should be to

> seek in the text itself, on the one hand, the internal dynamic that governs the structuring of the work and, on the other hand, the power that the work possesses to project itself outside itself and to give birth to a world that would truly be the "thing" referred to by the text. This internal dynamic and external projection constitute what I call the work of the text. It is the task of hermeneutics to reconstruct this twofold work. ("On Interpretation," 17–18)

When encountering texts of and on professional identity and careers in higher education, we are both the interpreter and, indeed, the "external work of the text." The rewards for our success at the task of interpretation are not only those of satisfying explication and understanding but also those potentially of personal and communal transformation.

Yet Ricoeur, like Gadamer, also expands dramatically what we even think of as "text" to include not only written narratives but also those that constitute our own lives and those of others whom we encounter. Indeed, a core tenet of Ricoeur's work, in line with my own argument here, is that we organize our lives as narratives and that the wide variety of other narratives we encounter have potentially enormous impact on our selves. As an example, he notes that "literature is a vast laboratory in which we experiment with estimations, evaluations, and judgments of approval and condemnation through which narrativity serves as a propaedeutic to ethics" (*Oneself*, 115). Yet this is not only true for what we deem "literature." As Karl Simms recognizes in his recent overview of Ricoeur's philosophy, Ricoeur's "hermeneutics becomes a theory of the text, which takes texts as its starting point, but ultimately comes to see the world as textual, insofar as human existence is expressed through discourse, and discourse is the invitation humans make to one another to be interpreted" (*Paul Ricoeur*, 31). We are both beings who are interpreted and also beings who are transformed through the process of interpreting others and their narratives: "In our experience the life history of each of us is caught up in the histories of others. Whole sections of my life are part of the life history of others—of my parents, my friends, my companions at work and in leisure" (Ricoeur, *Oneself*, 161). Our lives are narratives entangled with other narratives, all demanding interpretation and response, and leading, through their intersection, interaction, and critical engagement, to an ability to live differently and more ethically.

Ricoeur's *Oneself as Another* argues explicitly that our narrative interpretive abilities empower us and, at the same time, burden us with the responsibility for ethical action. He is not calling for a blind adherence to morals—static laws of proper behavior—but instead posits a process of living with ethical intent, which he defines as *"aiming at the 'good life' with and for others, in just institutions"* (*Oneself*, 172; original italics). While Ricoeur leaves unstated a precise definition for the terms he uses in that broad injunction, he clearly emphasizes the responsibility to work in community and with communal awareness toward more responsive interpersonal relations and self-reflective social/institutional structures.

This relates to narrative interpretation and incorporation in a striking way. Ricoeur demands from each of us a conscious, if always metamorphic, "life plan":

> We shall term "life plans" those vast practical units that make up professional life, family life, leisure time, and so forth. These life plans take shape—a shape that is mobile and, moreover, changeable—thanks to a back-and-forth movement between more or less distant ideals, which must now be specified, and the weighing of advantages and disadvantages of the choice of a particular life plan on the level of practices. (*Oneself*, 157–58)

He adds later, "between our aim of a 'good life' and our particular choices a sort of hermeneutical circle is traced by virtue of the back-and-forth motion between our idea of the 'good life' and the most important decisions of our existence (career, loves, leisure, etc.)" (179). This circle of broadly conceived but thoughtful life goals, sharpened and augmented by communal commentary, and then brought back into engagement with the practical matter of daily life, provides that measure of agency that both empowers us and makes us responsible for our actions and decisions.

And this, of course, differentiates Ricoeur's exploration of narrative modeling, interrogation, and incorporation from anything like a simple awe or replication of others' life plans, such as that promoted by some self-help books that suggest that we base our lives on those of successful individuals (often the author of the book itself). As critical, analytical, *thinking* beings, we have the responsibility to choose with care and, above all, with an overarching commitment to ethical treatment of others. Hitler's *Mein Kampf* and Machiavelli's *The Prince* may be inspirational narratives for some people, but are hardly ones that Ricoeur's philosophy would admit as acceptable if a just, diverse, and conversationally engaged community is held as the highest value.

In a similar vein, a half century ago, John F. Kennedy wrote in his *Profiles in Courage*, "To be courageous, these stories make clear, requires no exceptional qualifications, no magic formula, no special combination of time, place and circumstance. It is an opportunity that sooner or later is presented to all of us" (225). Kennedy recognized that his readers could not simply replicate the choices and life plans of his profiled politicians, but that it was useful for his readers to see how, at times, individuals can choose to place ideals above careerist self-interest. He was not offering formulas for successful living, but instead a range of examples of how others exercised agency in their own lives and made difficult choices about personal and professional priorities. He asks his readers to consider his profiled lives as ones lived with "integrity" (218), in which ethics are integrated into practices and ideals into daily decisions. Kennedy suggests that his stories of others' choices "can teach, they can offer hope, they can provide inspiration" (225). He, too, urged that we should always be the students of what we read.

I do not have the space here to offer the lengthy narratives and detailed analysis that Kennedy provided for his readers. However, I would like to offer a similar type of interpretive opportunity in microcosm. Profiled here briefly are five individuals, all but the first one employed in the academy, whose negotiation between broad conceptual commitments and the daily or otherwise concrete decisions that should flow from them, demonstrate the integrity mentioned above. I suppose one could say that they had or are having exceptional lives and careers, but the principles underlying those lives are ones that any of us can learn from. Their life plans, as I narrate them, certainly demand critical response, but it is precisely the human imperfection of them that demonstrates their potential applicability. Indeed, in humanizing them, we also should be better able to narrate, with a critical consciousness, our own professional selves to ourselves and to each other. The "us/them" divide in all of its pernicious manifestations (of importance or prestige, and of historical position or perspective, in this case) too often works simply to abet the status quo and justify passivity rather than the taking of responsibility.

George Eliot

The Victorian novelist George Eliot (Mary Ann Evans, 1819–1880) has long been a touchstone for me, for her social commentary, sense of communal responsibility, and vocational passion. She is the only one here who was not employed in higher education (except to the extent that she is regularly taught in universities), because such a career path was, of course, impossible for women during her era. Yet she pertains to our discussion, for in each of her novels, she explores the complex interplay of individual desire and that which constrains it, from Dinah Morris's socially transgressive public preaching in her first novel, *Adam Bede*, through Daniel Deronda's search for meaning and vocation in her last completed novel that bears his name.

Indeed, Eliot's reading of the interplay of the personal and contextual is captured beautifully in some of the closing words from her most acclaimed work, *Middlemarch*, as her narrator reflects on Dorothea Brooke's thwarted vocational ambitions:

> [The] determining acts of her life were not ideally beautiful. They were the mixed result of young and noble impulse struggling amidst the conditions of an imperfect social state, in which great feelings will often take the aspect of error, and great faith the aspect of illusion. For there is no creature whose inward being is so strong that it is not greatly determined by what

lies outside it. A new [Saint] Theresa will hardly have the opportunity of reforming a conventual life, any more than a new Antigone will spend her heroic piety in daring all for the sake of a brother's burial: the medium in which their ardent deeds took shape is forever gone. But we insignificant people with our daily words and acts are preparing the lives of many Dorotheas, some of which may present a far sadder sacrifice than that of the Dorothea whose story we know. (811)

This passage warrants several comments. One is that we cannot expect to succeed at vocational projects that are not in dialogue with the specific needs, values, and social beliefs of our era. No one can simply replicate the lives and life choices of a Saint Theresa, an Antigone, or, for that matter, a George Eliot.

However, Eliot is hardly hopeless about effective social action. She implies in the same quotation that we who make up the social and educational context of our contemporary Dorotheas, through "our daily words and acts," have the ability to make that context less oppressive and more supportive of intellectual innovation. There is, therefore, a pedagogical and broader social mandate contained in the passage. We are that which "lies outside" the "being" of our colleagues, students, and neighbors. Our words and acts can abet oppression and even tragedy, or they can help prepare better lives for others. Therefore, none of us is truly insignificant. Individually and collectively, we are responsible for communal transformation, even if as individuals we may find our goals and ideals thwarted at times. Certainly Eliot, herself, always persisted. She lived in an era in which women were not thought capable of writing philosophically rooted social criticism and intellectually challenging novels; Eliot nevertheless strategized to do so and publish under a pseudonym. Her monumental successes as a Victorian fiction writer and sage were the result of daily commitments and a decision to take the social situation into which she was born and challenge it with care and wisdom. While we cannot model our lives simply on Eliot's, any more than Dorothea could on Saint Theresa's, we are urged throughout Eliot's novels to find a task that is appropriate for us and for our time and to commit ourselves to it.

This is nowhere clearer than in the transformation of Daniel Deronda, who is at first a smart but directionless young man, but who re-creates himself as a social reformer committed to an international cause. Late in the novel, he tells the heretofore vain and foolish Gwendolyn Harleth:

> The idea that I am possessed with is that of restoring a political existence
> to my people, making them a nation again, giving them a national center,
> such as the English have, though they too are scattered over the face of the
> globe. That is a task which presents itself to me as a duty: I am resolved to
> begin it, however feebly. I am resolved to devote my life to it. At the least,
> I may awaken a movement in other minds, such as has been awakened in
> my own. (875)

Deronda's resolve to commit himself to a communal cause and a form
of consciousness-raising has an immediate effect on Gwendolyn: "[S]he
was for the first time feeling the pressure of a vast mysterious movement, for the first time being dislodged from her supremacy in her own
world, and getting a sense that her horizon was but a dipping onward of
an existence with which her own was revolving" (876). Not Deronda's
precise life plan, but rather his vocational commitment, is a model for
Gwendolyn of a life lived with purpose and passion. The result is a new
resolve in Gwendolyn too: "I shall live. I shall be better" (879). That
final determination is what Eliot asks of us as well. In Eliot's perspective,
such commitments always have a generative (even pedagogical) effect,
awakening in others (community members, students, or colleagues) a
similar resolve.

Friedrich Nietzsche

No one, perhaps, would seem more distant from Eliot philosophically
than Nietzsche. But if Eliot urges us to consider thoughtfully our lives in
the context of others and a world that needs ardent reform efforts, Friedrich Nietzsche (1844–1900) urges us to challenge conventions boldly
and create our lives as passionate works of art. Nietzsche demonstrated
enormous scholarly talents in his young adulthood and was appointed to
his first academic position in his early twenties, at the University of Basel.
He published his first book, *The Birth of Tragedy*, at age twenty-seven,
which was followed by many others, at rapid pace, until he withdrew
from academic life, ill and disenchanted, in his mid-thirties. His is not a

narrative of conventional academic success, by any means. Yet Nietzsche's iconoclasm has had its own generative effect that dovetails with Eliot's injunctions above. We create the communal conditions that either stifle or incite creativity and intellectual growth.

Indeed, Nietzsche persisted in following his own life project regardless of the negativity of others and the weight of the status quo. Throughout his career, he was severely criticized by his peers for his style of writing and the content of his books, yet he did not waver from his mission to challenge convention and change people's perceptions of the world. As one commentator, Lee Spinks notes, *The Birth of Tragedy* was the first of many of Nietzsche's books that was

> fiercely condemned by the academic community for its "unphilosophical" approach, although the shock that Nietzsche's work produced in intellectual circles was represented in more neutral terms as distaste for his violation of scholarly etiquette, abrupt shifts of historical focus and needlessly polemical tone. The stage was set for a dispute between Nietzsche and German intellectual culture that was to last the rest of his life. (*Friedrich Nietzsche*, 2–3)

Nietzsche is a case study in rebellion against academic norms that led to harsh responses, but that was pursued bravely nevertheless and in adherence to guiding ideals that included the reform of a scholarly discipline.

Indeed, in his *Unfashionable Observations* (1873–75), Nietzsche challenges directly the conservative nature of the research obsessions of his era:

> Antiquarian history degenerates from the moment when the fresh life of the present no longer animates and inspires it. At this point, piety withers, the scholarly habit persists without it and revolves with self-satisfied egotism around its own axis. Then we view the repugnant spectacle of a blind mania to collect, of a restless gathering together of everything that once existed. The human being envelops himself in the smell of mustiness. . . . Often he sinks so low that in the end he is satisfied with any fare and even devours with gusto the dust of bibliographical minutiae. (105)

In that passage, Nietzsche rebukes an academic and more general intellectual climate of lockstep conformity and obsessive inwardness. What he calls for instead, is a "critical mode" of academic work that seeks not to collect the past but to create the future:

> In order to live, he must possess, and from time to time employ, the strength to shatter and dissolve a past; he accomplishes this by bringing this past before a tribunal, painstakingly interrogating it, and finally condemning it. . . . [A]t times this very life that requires forgetfulness demands the temporary suspension of this forgetfulness; this is when it is supposed to become absolutely clear precisely how unjust the existence of certain things—for example, a privilege, a caste, or a dynasty—really is, and how much these things deserve to be destroyed. This is when its past is viewed critically, when we take a knife to its roots, when we cruelly trample on all forms of piety. (106–7)

These are incendiary words directed toward a moribund intellectual and academic culture. He asks us, even today, to energize our work with a vision for the future and thus champions the struggles of the innovative researcher, the social activist, and the pedagogical trailblazer. In *The Gay Science* (1882), Nietzsche urges his readers to "*live dangerously*. Build your cities on the slopes of Vesuvius! Send your ships into uncharted seas! Live at war with your peers and yourselves!" (228). Of course, he gives that advice from the position of someone who has already lived, and suffered the consequences of, such a commitment to iconoclasm. Yet Nietzsche asks us to persist even when the volcano threatens to erupt and destroy us. As practical advice, this may seem extreme (and highly problematic if our own dependants' lives and welfare is linked to our continued employment), but as a motivational tool and reminder of the trap of blind allegiance to the status quo, it is priceless.

Alexander Nehamas, in *Nietzsche: Life as Literature*, argues persuasively that Nietzsche demands from us a life lived with a conscious style and purpose:

> a person worthy of admiration, a person who has (or is) a self, is one whose thoughts, desires, and actions are not haphazard but are instead connected

to one another in the intimate way that indicates in all cases the presence of style. . . . [An] admirable self, as Nietzsche insists again and again,
consists of a large number of powerful and conflicting tendencies that are
controlled and harmonized. Coherence, of course, can also be produced
by weakness, mediocrity, and one-dimensionality. But style, which is
what Nietzsche requires and admires, involves controlled multiplicity and
resolved conflict. (7)

This is a highly conscious version of the overarching life plan that Ricoeur
also demands. While Nietzsche finally left the academy because of condemnation, ill-health, and disgust with the norms of his community, his
passion is worth attending to and learning from. Within our communities, we can bring Nietzsche's commitment to reform and creative thinking to bear in our work as teachers, researchers, and institutional citizens.
He reminds us that some life projects may be even more important than
a particular institutional position or set of career perks. Indeed, nothing
is more telling than the fact that Nietzsche continues to speak to us,
sparking skepticism and intellectual innovation, while his dust-devouring
colleagues are all silent.

Paul Ricoeur

Ricoeur's own life plan (1913–2005) offers an alternate vision and narrative, teaching that one can encounter an extraordinarily oppressive situation and yet persist in one's intellectual and pedagogical commitments.
Our departments or colleges may be dysfunctional or unsupportive, but
Ricoeur faced far more extreme circumstances and yet persisted in his
commitment to the creation of a supportive educational and research
community. When we think times are bad because our grant application
was turned down or a colleague acted disdainfully toward us, it is useful
to remember that our troubles are often minor indeed when placed in a
historical and global context.

Ricoeur was educated at the University of Rennes and the Sorbonne,
before he took secondary-school teaching positions in Colmar and Lorient
during the mid- to late 1930s, which he remembers as a time of great "success" and "happiness." But as he goes on to recount in an autobiographical

narrative, "The war caught me by surprise at the end of a beautiful summer spent with my wife at the University of Munich attending a German language class. I was, in turn, drafted civilian, then combatant, and finally vanquished combatant and imprisoned officer" ("Intellectual Autobiography," 9). His own modest narration of what happened during his five years in prisoner-of-war camps is of a "time of extraordinary human experiences: daily life, shared interminably with thousands of others, the cultivation of intense friendships, the regular rhythm of improvised instruction, of uninterrupted stretches of reading those books available in the camp" (9). Ricoeur read the recently published work of Karl Jaspers, a German, whom he later thanks personally "for having placed my admiration for German thinking outside of the reach of all of the negative aspects of our surroundings and of the 'terror of history'" (9). That act of acknowledgment certainly demonstrates a generosity of spirit that is noteworthy.

But Ricoeur's intellectual and pedagogical commitments led to more than simply an ambitious reading plan. Many critics mentioning those five years of captivity rush past them (presumably in an attempt to get to what commentators would consider Ricoeur's "real work"), but a few provide more detail. According to Karl Simms, Ricoeur, after being captured,

> helped set up an unofficial "University of the Prison Camp," where a group of prisoners would lecture to one another and collaborate in research. It was difficult to get hold of books other than German ones, and thus it was that Ricoeur read the work of the German philosopher Edmund Husserl . . . for the first time, and translated Husserl's most famous book, *Ideas* (1913), into French. Despite conditions of dreadful hardship (which included there being scarcely any paper available), Ricoeur also began a book on the German Christian existentialist philosopher Karl Jaspers . . . , co-written with a fellow prisoner, Mikel Dufrenne, and a comparative study of Jaspers and Marcel. (*Paul Ricoeur*, 3)

As Charles Reagan notes, "intellectually, those years were not wasted, even though the surroundings were depressing and basic human needs were only minimally met" (*Paul Ricoeur*, 10).

That is an understatement, of course. Imprisoned, facing brutal conditions and possibly death, Ricoeur found ways to live his commitment to education and intellectual exchange.

> The "university within the camp" began almost immediately, during the summer of 1940. Paul-André Lesort reports that Ricoeur gave a "Lecture on Nietzsche" on July 17. . . . As the war as well as their imprisonment dragged on, the "university" became better organized, with more regular courses aimed at replicating an academic year. By 1943, they had received permission from the minister of education in Vichy to give examinations, and later, after the war was over, the French government validated some of the university degrees earned in the camp. (Reagan, *Paul Ricoeur*, 10)

Not only did Ricoeur and others work as instructors in their makeshift university, they also worked as its administrators and support staff. All the while, they were contending with terrible conditions. Some prisoners who attempted to escape were killed; everyone was suffering from the cold and lack of adequate food.

The question I raise to myself as I read a narrative such as the one above is *what do I believe I would have done under the same circumstances and how are those ideals reflected in what I am doing now?* What intellectual and pedagogical commitments can any of us articulate that will help us make intellectually productive and communally responsible choices under difficult conditions? Our challenges are usually far less extreme than those faced by Ricoeur and his fellow prisoners, yet we all know academics who complain ad nauseam about having to settle for older-model computers in their offices, poorly stocked libraries, and unsupportive administrative structures. I am not saying that we should accept oppressive circumstances or ignore injustices. Yet I would argue that the responsibility that all of us share is to take the situations that we find ourselves in, add value to them, shape them to the extent that we can to meet our intellectual and pedagogical commitments, leave them if we find them intolerable, but above all, expend our energy "*aiming at the 'good life' with and for others, in just institutions,*" to the extent that we can create that good life and those just institutions. That life project should allow no time for sulking, whining, bitterness, envy, or destructive activities toward others.

To resort to a cliché, life is simply too short. As soon as Ricoeur was released, he immediately resumed teaching, threw himself into his writing, and soon established in his home a famous "Sunday afternoon" teaching and discussion circle that welcomed students, colleagues, and visitors to drop in and wrangle over the issues of the day. His ideals remained consistent whatever his circumstances. Throughout his career, Ricoeur worked indefatigably to help shape the conditions under which his own intellectual life and personal life, and those of others, could thrive. I hope I remember always to try to do the same.

Angela Davis

Angela Davis (1944–), now professor in the History of Consciousness Program at the University of California, Santa Cruz, has also lived a life in which theory and practice, social consciousness, and pedagogical intensity have been stunningly integrated, and in her case, even at the risk of her life. From her childhood in Birmingham, Alabama, during the worst years of racist terrorism by some members of the white population, to undergraduate studies at Brandeis, and then graduate study at UC San Diego and in Europe, Davis always used the narratives that she read—whether of fiction or philosophy—to critique her immediate context and as the basis for the day-to-day decisions that she made. As she studied and found that she substantially agreed with the writings of Karl Marx on class oppression, it was impossible for her to ignore Marx as she made decisions in her daily life, especially concerning the need to integrate the theoretical and the practical. Thus, even as she worked toward her PhD, she struggled to balance activism, teaching, and writing:

> It was a great relief to learn that I had done quite well on the [PhD qualifying] examinations. Having passed them, I began to work on the prospectus for my dissertation, and became a teaching assistant in the Philosophy Department, a further requirement for the PhD. About half of each week I spent researching and teaching in La Jolla and the other half I devoted to my political work in Los Angeles. (*Autobiography*, 190)

While she was later writing her dissertation (sometimes "work[ing] from one or two A.M. until six or seven" [*Autobiography*, 275]), she also balanced teaching classes at the University of California, Los Angeles, and taking a leadership role in mobilizing her community to support prisoner rights. Whether you agree or disagree with all of her premises and actions, hers is an intellectual and academic life lived with a degree of integrity that is extraordinary.

Indeed, she retained her commitment to her ideals despite enormous risks and costs. While working on prison reform and teaching at UCLA, she "was daily receiving multiple death threats. Campus police provided some measure of protection as she taught classes and met with students [while friends] and co-activists provided off-campus security" (James, *Angela Y. Davis Reader,* 10). Her work with the Communist Party on prison reform issues eventually cost her that teaching post; the UC regents first fired her for her party membership and, when that was ruled unconstitutional, fired her a second time for giving "political speeches outside the classroom [that] were 'unbefitting a university professor'" (*Autobiography,* 273). Her controversial work soon led to trumped-up charges as an accessory to murder, a nationwide manhunt, and her inclusion on the FBI's 10 Most Wanted List. Yet, even after being captured in New York, her sixteen-month incarceration provided her with new opportunities for teaching and consciousness-raising; she started workshops with other inmates on radical philosophy and devoted herself to writing on social justice issues (which culminated in her first book). Indeed, her determination to take the extreme conditions at hand, and do with them what she could to continue her teaching and research, is as much a model for us as Ricoeur's activities were during World War II. Both moved from classroom, to incarceration, and then back to the classroom after being released. After her acquittal, Davis taught for many years at San Francisco State University before accepting an appointment as Presidential Chair at UC Santa Cruz (and in doing so, proving wrong Ronald Reagan's statement when he was governor that Davis would "never" teach in California again). At UCSC, she has, among many other projects, "developed writing groups for students, a lecture series involving cross-racial conversations, colloquia, [and] meetings with the Women of Color Resource Center in Oakland" ("Reflections," 319). Raised by two teachers in a community that valued education as a means for social advancement, Davis "was persuaded very early in [her] life that liberation was not possible without education" ("Reflections," 316). From that life plan, she has never wavered.

Indeed, Davis's legacy will surely be one of exceptionally brave intellectual engagement. Davis herself used her dissertation director, Herbert Marcuse, as a model, saying that he "not only theorized" but also "actively participated in mobilizations both in the United States and Europe." She continues, "Working so closely with him during that period, I learned that while teaching and agitation were very different practices, students need to be assured that politics and intellectual life are not two entirely different modes of existence. I learned that I did not have to leave political activism behind to be an effective teacher ("Reflections," 318). Theory and practice are integrated for Davis in ways that I deeply admire. While her causes are not my causes, hers is a degree of commitment against which I can judge my own. Indeed, few of us may find our cause in radical political activism, yet all of us will be presented with choices daily about whether or not our lives reflect our theories. Davis writes in the introduction to her autobiography that in working on it, "I did not measure the events of my own life according to their possible personal importance. Rather I attempted to utilize the autobiographical genre to evaluate my life in accordance with what I considered to be the political significance of my experiences" (*Autobiography*, viii). She offers her story because "there was the possibility that, having read it, more people would understand why so many of us have no alternative but to offer our lives—our bodies, our knowledge, our will—to the cause of our oppressed people" (xvi). Indeed, that is one version of the modeling that I am calling for here. If we think of ourselves in this way, as texts to be read, critiqued, and possibly emulated, then we may be spared the ever-present, ever-possible trap of academic solipsism.

Hans-Georg Gadamer

Gadamer's work is at the heart of this book's argument, and while I'll reference his theories throughout upcoming chapters, I do want to reflect a bit on his life as one possible model for our academic work and engagements. In his autobiographical narrative, *Philosophical Apprenticeships*, Gadamer devotes chapters to each of the major philosophers whom he encountered as a student and philosopher-in-training, and traces generously what he learned from these mentors. He does there what we are doing here: isolating the central commitments of a professional life and examining them critically for their use value in the life that he was constructing. In the philosopher Hans Lipps, for example, he discovered a "resolute original," who had an "impetuous manner with which he applied himself to his conversation partner: without restraint, without flourish, totally concentrated" (89); in Max Scheler he found a passionate lecturer and intellectual whose "reading so devoured him that whenever he met a colleague he would compel his participation simply by ripping pages out of whatever book he was reading and pressing them into the hands of his astonished companion" (33); about Martin Heidegger he writes "the unique thing about his person and his teaching lay in the fact that he identified himself fully with his work and radiated from that work. . . . What he provided was the full investment of his energy, and what brilliant energy it was" (48). Out of these and many other scripts of a teaching and intellectual life, Gadamer constructed his own life plan.

And what might we learn from that life and life plan? Gadamer's was the energy of steady professional and intellectual transformation built on a thorough but always critical knowledge of what had gone before. As a novice teacher, he experienced the worries that all of us do as we begin a career: "The beginning of every semester was filled with anxiety: Would the chosen theme prove seaworthy? And would I prove able to sail it to the opposite shore?" (70). He admits, "At the podium I was very shy, and I heard later that people occasionally characterized me as follows: 'Oh, there he is, the one who never looks up'" (71). But over time he hones his pedagogy, learns from colleagues, and finally becomes a popular teacher and a leader of faculty. While never objectifying other human beings, he nevertheless examined them as texts of sorts, as complex conveyers of meaning whom he must interpret and from whom he can learn. This is clearly a putting into lived practice his own theory of hermeneutics, which provided a coherence and honesty to a life filled with intellectual passion and a generous commitment to community.

Thus even in the darkest days of World War II, Gadamer found ways to subvert the curricular censorship of the Nazis and continue to teach his courses

> amidst increasing destruction. We read our lectures in emergency rooms set up in the university library, from which books had been removed and which had so far been spared bombing. . . . Unforgettable to me is the smell of burnt paper, which I perceived one February morning in 1945 and just as quickly diagnosed. The Central Security Office, which had been moved

from Berlin to Leipzig and installed in a castle in the vicinity of my house, was burning its files. This was a breath of fresh air. We had survived. (101)

Gadamer was not a radical political activist like Angela Davis, nor was he a prison camp subversive like his (later) friend Paul Ricoeur. He simply taught his classes under terrible circumstances and attempted to awaken in his students the critical abilities to judge for themselves in an oppressive context. Of course, there is no one perfect or exclusive model of success or professional responsibility. If we think that only those people who take to the streets or attempt to overturn wholly previous notions or paradigms are the brave and successful ones, then we will probably feel like failures. Those of us who do important and difficult work in classrooms and in administrative meetings have every reason to feel proud of the microlevel impact that we have on our students' and colleagues' lives. Gadamer as institutional citizen, not as world-famous philosopher, offers us a narrative from which to learn.

After the war, Gadamer committed himself to the daily work that was needed: "The American occupation passed undramatically, and the preparation for the reorganization of the university fell for the most part to me" (103). He soon learned, "I would be the rector [president] chosen to reopen the university. I was duly elected and now began the exhausting, interesting, illusion-rich, and disillusioning work of construction—or was it deconstruction?—of Leipzig University" (104). Indeed, how many of us, given the currently fashionable scorn of administrators in the American academy, would shoulder that same burden? In the middle of an intellectual career of incredible, but still largely unrealized potential (his major works were published when he was in his sixties), Gadamer, in his mid-forties, chose to devote himself to the mundane and hard work of institutional reform and leadership. While I will discuss other aspects of his institutional life in later chapters, I offer part of his narrative here because Gadamer's devotion to his community, at the temporary expense of his own research and writing, may make him a particularly compelling role model for some readers contemplating a department chairship, a university leadership role, or some other time-consuming assignment. He has served that purpose for me, several times.

● ● ●

What do we do with these professional narratives or with the many others that we encounter regularly (and, in fact, we may have heard equally or even more compelling life narratives from our own mentors, relatives, or friends)? We should treat them as richly instructive texts from which we can glean important, even vital, information about how we might (not should, but might) lead our own lives. Some of us already seek advice from career counselors or consult books on writing grants or getting published. But there are much broader, meta-ontological questions that we can find partial, sometimes idiosyncratic, answers to by attending carefully and critically to the life stories and professional and personal narratives of colleagues and mentors. As I indicated earlier, this should not be tantamount to hero worship, nor should it simply replicate a 1980s star system that swathed a few successful academic writers in an aura of glamour, but with no discussion of the intensely hard work and microlevel choices and practices that led to their fleeting success. In fact, while my narratives above are of very well-known individuals, what I hope to impress upon readers is that these individuals' lives involved mundane choices about goals and priorities that all of us face on a daily basis. Fame is only a chance by-product of what should be a life lived with critical awareness of our own needs and talents, in negotiation with those of our family members, friends, students, and colleagues.

And while teleological thinking has been aptly criticized by social constructionist thinkers for its oversimplicity and reductive idealism, there is still something to be said for choosing to ascribe importance to certain thoughtful aims or goals in life. One way of thinking about this dynamic, which an administrator I know uses as a motivational technique, is to consider what legacy you would like to leave as a teacher, scholar, administrator, and/or colleague. Some deride the exercise, but in my opinion, articulating to yourself or others what you hope to accomplish in order to leave your department, college, or university a better place when you leave or retire is not an intellectually shallow activity. It is, rather, to assume responsibility for the communal consequences of individual actions and decisions.

"Legacy" thinking forces us to consider our personal interests as ones intertwined with the lives, careers, and happiness of others. In approaching our own lives as narratives, with certain themes that we wish to emphasize and a certain import that we wish to have linger after the narrative's close, we take ourselves temporarily "out" of ourselves. We perform a "meta-" movement that while always incomplete, flawed, and tendentious nevertheless is absolutely necessary for ethical and communally responsible behavior. If we cannot test our actions in department meetings, in hallway exchanges with students or colleagues, and in our demands for "special treatment," against larger principles and desired communal outcomes, our lives will always be lived with narrow forms of self-interest in the predominate position. Granted, to decide to leave a legacy of generosity and communal transformation may be termed a "self-interested" act—what is more vain than wanting to be thought of, after one's retirement or death, as a wonderful, generous person?—but there is no escape from that charge by cynics and other individuals committed to justifying the status quo. As I stated in *The Academic Self,* I am not religious (though I certainly respect those who are) and am generally uncomfortable with all transcendental ascriptions of life meaning, so all I have are the choices that I make as I live my daily life and seek forms of contentment in my family (of blood relatives and of choice), my community, and my work. My wish is that all of us choose wisely and with love and respect for those around us.

And this in turn means that we have to think of our life narrative as one always potentially judged by others for its utility as a model. That places even greater responsibility on us for choosing wisely and well. It is far too simplistic to reduce this to a simple Kantian imperative of choosing in every instance as if one's choice were to become a universal maxim. Life is too complicated for that and some choices in one's personal life (eating too many brownies on occasion) are not ones that necessarily have to concern others. But in choosing one's career and communal goals, and in deciding how best to integrate one's values and one's interrelationships, there is a certain quasi-Kantian thought process that has to go on. Am I choosing selfishly or am I choosing in a way that places broader needs and interests in active conversation with my own? Am I choosing to live my academic life in a way that I would wish my own students to emulate? These questions do not mandate clear-cut rules or litmus tests, but do disrupt what can be an automatic reversion to self-interest as the basis for our demands on our colleagues, institutions, and administrators. In thinking of ourselves as *potential* texts and role models for others, we are at least offered a check on, or disruption of, the always present potential for solipsism that accompanies a life of, and in, the mind.

Yet to take ourselves out of ourselves in that way is not to diminish the importance that we should ascribe to our activities and professional goals. Our work may never revolutionize thinking worldwide, as Nietzsche's did, or inspire international human rights campaigns, as Davis's did. However, our impact in our own spheres of influence and in our own communities can be just as powerful, and certainly the passion and seriousness that we bring to our projects and goals can be as intense for us as it was for any of the intellectuals mentioned earlier. My books will never reach the numbers of readers that Eliot's did and will never change fields of study the ways that Paul Ricoeur's did, but I am absolutely certain that the intensity of the writing experience for me is as powerful as it was for them.

A mistake that many of us make is to think that our teaching, our research, and our work in our communities are not important or sufficiently consequential. That diminishment of our work (either overtly expressed or simply covertly felt) leads us to envy others, provides an easy excuse for procrastination, and feeds inertia, bitterness, and a sense of failure. Indeed, our attitude toward the importance of our vocational plans and projects can take on the dynamic of a self-fulfilling prophecy—our work becomes unimportant and limited in its impact because we think that it can only be that.

What I hope to accomplish in this book is to challenge and change that negative thinking and overly circumscribed planning. The microcosms of our programs, departments, colleges, and universities demand the same ardent attention that others have devoted to larger organizations and better-known institutions. It may sound absurd to suggest that we treat our programmatic reforms at the department level with the same seriousness that others are devoting to reforms at the United Nations, but on a phenomenological level, I have no doubt that the two can evoke similar emotions and anxieties. Both matter immensely because they represent two manifestations of that striving for a good life with and for others, in just institutions. Thus when I get out of bed in the morning and contemplate my day, whether it is devoted to writing on professional matters or meeting with colleagues or both, I search for and usually find that sense of passion and commitment about what will comprise my day that I know from memoirs and other self-expressions of work life that others have felt in vocations usually deemed much more important or consequential.

And that returns me to my point about a form of hermeneutics that allows us to think of our "selves" as narrative works in progress, to step outside of those narratives with reference to those of others, and to return to our life plans and imagined legacies with a renewed vigor and assumption of agency. In Ricoeur's words, "we learn to become the *narrator of our own story* without completely becoming the author of our life" ("Life," 437; original italics). In saying this, he revises the philosophical observation mentioned earlier: "We are [now] led to say that a life *examined*, in the sense borrowed from Socrates, is a life *narrated*" ("Life," 435; original italics). As we narrate those lives to each other, judiciously to students, and with all possible honesty to ourselves, we must continue to revisit and revise them in dialogue: with the life narratives of other intellectuals, with the needs and desires of our partners, children, colleagues, and students, and with our own concrete projections of what we would like to accomplish and how our daily activities do or do not help us meet those goals. Gadamer writes in his own dialogue with Ricoeur, "We can objectify ourselves; we can decipher the text of our own life, seeing it as a full series of symptoms of an illusion. Yet how can we make our way through this in a way that does justice to concrete life as an interpretive process? For me the pre-eminent model has been the *dialogue*" (Ricoeur, "Conflict," 222).

The passion that we bring to narrating our academic lives is the passion of creation, but creation with communal awareness and communal, even critical, commentary. In narrating the text of our professional lives within a broader dynamic of response and revision, we are all allowed relational points of reference that then return us to the texts of our lives with an ability to alter them. We may not be the "author" of our own lives, but we make choices every day in ways that constitute the text of those lives. We can choose openness.

chapter two

. . . .

Empowering Student
Intellectuals

$\mathcal{W}$ HETHER WE in the academy self-define most emphatically
as researchers, undergraduate teachers, program administrators,
or through some combination of these and other roles, our primary professional responsibility is always education. This may sound like a truism to
some of my readers, but I'm not sure that all of our colleagues would agree.
Former Cornell University president Frank H. T. Rhodes notes with regret
that "a generation or two ago, a professor at a major university would have
described himself as a professor or an educator; today, such an individual
is likely to describe herself as an engineer, an architect, or a musicologist,
and, if pressed, to say that she teaches at such-and-such university" (*Creation of the Future*, 61). While, unlike Rhodes, I have little nostalgia for
yesterday's ways of professing, I agree with him that it is crucial for us to
remember that even if we sequester ourselves in an office or a laboratory
and spend our days and nights working to generate new knowledge about
plant biology or artificial intelligence, we do so finally only as a precur-
sor to transmitting that new knowledge to others: through publication,
through conversation or oral presentation, and through teaching in the
classroom. Indeed, as administrators managing the budget of a college
or department chairs overseeing hiring and tenuring processes for large
groups of faculty, if we do not define our roles as ones of educating and
mentoring others—students, other faculty, and the public at large—then

we will likely be ineffective and irresponsible in those roles.

Later chapters of this book will examine a wide variety of venues in which we act as educators and mentors, but I want to begin here with the one that is the most common across the landscape of our profession though it often receives little attention in books devoted specifically to academic professional studies: the undergraduate classroom. Every person reading this book who holds an academic position has been an under-graduate and most will teach undergraduates regularly. The community of undergraduates with whom we interact is usually larger than any other community with whom we have regular contact, except the public at large. As we become agents of change in all of our academic communi-ties, our actions and interactions as teachers of undergraduates is a logical place to begin.

Yet certainly at PhD-granting institutions, undergraduate education is seen often as an unpleasant necessity rather than a core mission and field of intense intellectual engagement. For many professors, graduate courses are regarded as the "prize" assignments, and undergraduate courses a punishment of sorts. No wonder students at many of our largest and most prestigious universities complain that they never get to work with or even meet the best-known faculty on their campuses. This is a state of neglect that may have dire consequences. We are doing our undergradu-ates and our own profession a disservice if we fail to engage in the work of undergraduate teaching with energy and enthusiasm. That enormous population will be the voting public (and pool of potential donors) whose financial support is crucial to the survival of our public institutions. But even more important, their thoughtful and knowledgeable contribu-tion to their own professions and, especially, to the public sphere could determine our collective survival. Every ethically and critically engaged undergraduate whom we help train is potentially one more individual who can work to find creative solutions to seemingly intractable inter-national conflicts and looming environmental crises. This is a cause for which all members of our profession should feel both intellectual passion and a sense of social and intellectual urgency.

I am not at all hesitant to call myself an enthusiastic teacher of under-graduates, and for those of us who do engage with passion in undergradu-ate education, "What do I want my undergraduate students to learn?" is a question with which we often grapple. While the precise answer depends upon the specific content of a given course, I want to take a more "macro" approach here. In fact, I believe it is crucial first to ask, "What are we already doing well, and what successes can we build upon?"

I have had several extended stays teaching at universities abroad: I was a visiting professor at the National University of Rwanda for two years in the mid-1980s (working with the Peace Corps) and then held a Fulbright Chair in Cultural Studies at Karl Franzens University in Graz, Austria, for half a year in 2005. I have lectured and taught classes at the University of Helsinki, the University of Zurich, and other places. One of the reasons I have sought out, and strongly advocate, such international experiences is because they allow a hermeneutic perspective, of the sort that I discussed earlier. By putting the U.S. system of higher education into conversation with the highly diverse international system of higher education, we can develop a multilayered perspective on what we are doing well in the United States and also what needs improvement.

I believe several commendations are warranted. Generally, our students already write more often, more voluminously, and more skillfully than students in many other educational systems across the globe. In Graz, many of my graduate students in the American Studies program struggled to write the first twenty-page paper they had ever been assigned. In their fifth and sixth years at the university, many had the composition abilities (even discounting language skill problems, of course) of American freshmen. No one had ever taught them the basics of organizing and supporting an extended piece of critical analysis. Even more tellingly, they were wholly untrained in challenging the authority of the writers whom they read and the theorists whom we were referencing. We in U.S. higher education already teach our students to think and write with considerable independence of thought, and that is a strength that we can build upon.

Similarly, and perhaps not surprisingly, both my graduate students and many undergraduates in Rwanda and in Graz also struggled to find a voice in my classes, since most had encountered only traditional lectures in the past. I succeeded in getting them to express opinions contrary to the textbooks or ones even simply questioning my own assertions only by breaking them into small groups and assigning them a sort of "devil's advocacy" role that they found unusual and at first very uncomfortable (though one they soon approached with enthusiasm). Upon returning to the States, I noted again how our students are far more active participants in the classroom and are far less reticent at challenging the perspectives of their teachers and peers. While our students' knowledge base vis-à-vis world events may be thin in comparison to their European and African counterparts, their ability to engage critically with each other, with popular culture, and with the latest trends in technology and identity-political issues is much sharper. Indeed, to any pundits or politicians who would bemoan multiculturalism and the exploration of diverse historical perspectives that students are exposed to in secondary schools, I would respond that many of these students emerge with a useful and, I will argue below, highly practical skepticism regarding the truth of received or "common" knowledge. When they arrive at universities, they often already possess nascent critical thinking skills that, when honed, will help them succeed personally and vocationally.

Finally, our universities' commitment to serving students' needs (with support services, advising centers, and student affairs offices) is well in advance of most other national systems. Graz, though a prestigious university with an ancestry dating back many centuries, had no central registration system, no central grade collection system, and no student services center. Furthermore, though many U.S. faculty complain about the time-consuming nature of outcomes assessment in our programs, we in American higher education clearly care enough about the skills and knowledge with which our students are exiting our colleges and universities to devote considerable time and energy to assessment processes. We attempt, sometimes successfully and sometimes not, to link the curriculum that we offer and that vision that we have of what a university education should *do* for students. Both curriculum and vision can be chaotic in many parts of the world. Our devotion to meeting our students' many needs is truly commendable, and we have an emerging but still globally unique base in outcomes assessment upon which to build.

Yet those successes and laudable qualities are only beginnings and should spur us to engage with our undergraduates even more productively and with our own roles and expectations as teachers even more critically. What we already do well is to begin to nurture in our students an independence of thought and an ability to engage in critical dialogue with others. Our challenges at present and for the future can be largely addressed by building forthrightly on those strengths. But we have to prioritize that work and assume responsibility for it. If we are unimpressed by our students' knowledge of world events and ability to react critically to international issues and America's role in the world, then who has more of an obligation than we do in higher education for remedying that situation? If we find that our students too often resort to clichés and hackneyed phrases when asked to reflect critically on social issues or their own lives, then who has more responsibility than we do in the academy for addressing that hastiness? If we as professionals are aware of our own lives as comprised of narratives adopted critically and judged forthrightly against broader vocational and personal ideals, then who better than we to inculcate the same critical faculties in our students? To complain vaguely about the failures of primary and secondary education systems, as is too often the case now, about the supposedly deadening influence of popular or visual culture, or about the general disrespect for intellectuals in the United States, gets us nowhere. We have a venue for social transformation—the classroom—and possess the skills necessary to help effect transformation.

But the question remains, what precise sort of transformation do we wish to prioritize? I suggest here that we build on the bases mentioned above, and work always and explicitly toward empowering our students with the critical and intellectual skills that will allow them to respond analytically to the many texts surrounding them—in print, in life, and in the media. Indeed, they should be encouraged to textualize their own life plans and to use those plans as a basis for conversation with other students, contemporary writers and thinkers, and cultural expressions from the past. Linking all of the work that teachers of undergraduates do in their classes—from the natural sciences to the humanities to the social sciences, mathematics, and engineering—is a common goal: inculcating in students the ability to respond knowledgeably and critically to the texts comprising their field of study and nurturing in them the passion needed to contribute to those fields skillfully and inventively. To put it another way: we must ask our students first *to demonstrate a solid base of knowledge in a given subject or field,* and then, *to add responsibly and creatively to the ongoing conversation comprising that subject or field.*

There is no "major" course of study or vocational track to which this broadly defined project does not pertain: as future accountants, educators, advertising executives, small business owners, teachers, engineers, financial planners, and research scientists, our students' success in life and in their careers will always depend upon their ability to understand, and choose wisely among, voices of authority and traditional ways of "doing," and then to innovate knowledgeably in negotiation with those authorities and traditions. In his essay "The Tasks of the Political Educator," Paul Ricoeur reminds us that "all the values of the past cannot survive; only those can which are susceptible to . . . reinterpretation" (292). Indeed, that is how Ricoeur defines a "political educator," one who facilitates that reinterpretation, which is not only fundamental to personal empowerment and economic prosperity, but also to social justice and global political stability.

And what is true for "values" is also true for knowledge bases generally. A static relationship with any field of knowledge and especially that comprising one's profession or vocation is deadly. One's ability to respond with intellectual courage and nuance has implications for career training and advancement, and far beyond. These are life skills and are the impulse behind the concept of "lifelong learning" as it has emerged to address the predicament of midcareer individuals who are unable to react flexibly to changing circumstances and whose careers have languished or ended because of that calcification. In empowering our students with those career skills, we empower them also in their personal, social, and political lives. In reframing our national conversation about the desired outcomes of higher education to focus specifically on "knowledge," "responsibility," and "innovation," we also train a citizenry that is more knowledgeable, responsible, and creative in its thinking about our nation and its place in a global conversation.

In focusing on such well-informed, responsible, and innovative reinterpretation of knowledge bases, I am unabashedly suggesting that we make the explicit aim of undergraduate education the creation of a new generation of intellectuals. I realize well that this term has a long and complicated history in the United States. In his still all-too-relevant book from 1962, *Anti-Intellectualism in American Life*, Richard Hofstadter writes, "Our anti-intellectualism is, in fact, older than our national identity. . . . The common strain that binds together the attitudes which I call anti-intellectual is a resentment and suspicion of the life of the mind and of those who are considered to represent it; and a disposition constantly to minimize the value of that life" (6–7). By necessity, then, given student demands for vocational training and the American suspicion of "thought for thought's sake," this must be a practical, real-life intellectualism, rather than an abstract or solely theoretical one.

That distinction is one that we can assert clearly in relating knowledge, responsibility, and innovation to the career interests of students and to practical social issues facing American society today. We must assert forcefully and unequivocally the value of thinking creatively and conversing with others before acting rashly. We must reclaim the value of knowledge, responsibility, and creativity in a political and social climate that too often values bombast and unsupported assertion, and suffers deadly consequences for such rashness. Activists working toward sexual justice and freedom successfully reclaimed the word "queer" in the early 1990s; I worked in the service of that campaign and have appreciated its limited but still significant successes. But queer theory and queer self-identity are only subsets of much more far-reaching critical intellectual work. Queer activism invited into its campaign all who oppose traditional templates of heterosexual privilege. A form of practical, real-life intellectualism as an ongoing life process and project (and not a set of prescribed beliefs or predetermined outcomes) has even broader possibilities for coalition-building and social transformation.

Indeed, this is one of the pedagogical imperatives that I glean from the work of Michel Foucault, who is still largely unreferenced in academic professional studies: to train a new generation of (in his terminology) "specific intellectuals," who find possibilities for critical engagement and innovative thinking in her or his sphere of "life and work, linked to his [or her] condition of employment" ("Truth and Power," 131–32). In Foucault's words, such intellectualism "does not consist in saying that things aren't good the way they are. It consists in seeing on what type of assumptions, of familiar notions, of established, unexamined ways of thinking the accepted practices are based. . . . [It] is to make harder those acts which are now too easy" ("So Is It Important to Think?" 456). Yet in saying that, Foucault never implies that it is sufficient simply to create a generation of contrarians or impractical iconoclasts. His is a call for skepticism in the service of innovation, and for intellectual productivity to replace mindless repetition and social stagnation. In short, it is to nurture and acquire the critical skills necessary for individual, institutional, vocational, and broad social change. Foucauldian specific intellectualism is a practical, real-world intellectualism.

In asking our students to find a vocational passion, a projected life plan, and a venue where they can commit themselves to do that specific and practical intellectual work, we are training a generation of students who understand their field(s) of study as ongoing conversations, and then add knowledgeably, responsibly, and creatively to those conversations. Indeed, my own thoughts on this topic have been formulated in conversation with other recent voices in the field of progressive pedagogy. In the remainder of this chapter, I want to focus on one that addresses undergraduate education in ways that I find laudable and that extols conversation even as it also warrants its own rejoinders.

Near the beginning of *Clueless in Academe*, Gerald Graff remarks, "Professors have been trained to think of [their students'] cluelessness as an uninteresting negative condition, a lack or a blank space to be filled in by superior knowledge" (5). His implication here and throughout the book is that arrogant and consistently disengaged academics are, in fact, the truly clueless individuals in academe. Graff addresses all of us teaching in the academy (even if the examples used to substantiate his diagnoses and flesh out his remedies are drawn from composition classrooms primarily), and, indeed, here as elsewhere, I read Graff's narrative for its truth value vis-à-vis my own commitments and pedagogy, as well as the work of others similarly invested in a version of Ricoeur's and Foucault's critical-thinking-based pedagogy. Frankly, I am a little skeptical about the bleakness and ubiquity of the problem he diagnoses, though at the same time I think he offers many suggestions that will help us build upon the strengths that I mentioned earlier.

To be sure, not all of our pedagogies are consistently student-centered and dynamic; however, I do think it is fair to say that most of us in higher education today would not find our students' "cluelessness" (if we adopt Graff's term) an *uninteresting* condition; it is, rather, what often piqued our initial interest in the teaching profession and is actually something with which we engage quite passionately within the microcosm of the classroom. In fact, that shift in underlying premise, in which we assume a passionate interest instead of lack thereof as our starting point, allows us then to appreciate many of Graff's suggestions while also refining them for our own use.

Even so, "cluelessness" is a term with which I want to engage critically for a moment. Graff defines it initially as "the bafflement, usually accompanied by shame and resentment, felt by students, the general public, and even many academics in the face of the impenetrability of the academic world" (1). Yet I am not sure that this is as profound a problem as Graff implies. The vast system of higher education in the United States, which includes community colleges and teaching-intensive universities (where I have spent most of my career to date), does not always, or even usually, baffle its students or the public. When colleges and universities add clear value to their students' lives and can explain to the public how its programs help students realize their own life plans and vocational goals, no one (or almost no one) is baffled. As head of advising for an English department at a teaching-intensive university in California for seven years and then chair of that department for two more years, no one expressed bafflement to me (other than occasionally over the confusing general education requirements that the university had in place at the time). Graff serves as a reminder, of course, that in those venues where students and the public *are* baffled, we have a crisis that needs addressing immediately. Serving the public more enthusiastically will be the topic of a later chapter, but using Graff as a stepping-stone, I suggest here that we reframe our pedagogical work to make sure that we do add clear and clearly explainable value to all of our undergraduates' lives.

Indeed, Graff's book does have much to tell us about the work that we do—and could do better—in the undergraduate classroom; many of his basic injunctions concerning the conversational energy that makes for good teaching and its most important payoff—the honing of students' critical thinking skills—are timely and relevant for all teachers. Graff urges us to make the classroom an exciting conversational and analytical venue. My own experience teaching gay and lesbian studies courses and content material in a variety of classes bears out the wisdom of his advice. There, even as basic premises of the class, are the rejection of formulae and a conversational engagement with static versions of truth held as core values, indeed, as microsocial and macrosocial "goods." And if Graff is accurate in saying that "Johnny can't argue" (155) in some of his classes, I know from experience that Johnny often has something to say when he encounters a film or literary representation of two men kissing passionately or two women living a domestic and sexual life with no need for Johnny's presence.

This is certainly not to suggest that all teachers have to work queer-relevant content into their classes, but it is to say that in finding material that immediately brings to the forefront student preconceptions and unexamined allegiances to traditional definitions, we have a singular opportunity to ask them to do the hard work of critically engaging with what they have been taught (or otherwise absorbed) to date, and to find ways of either marshaling evidence to support their beliefs (evidence that will itself stand up to critical scrutiny and communal examination) or to modify their beliefs in the service of an expansion of knowledge and as a creative addition to an ongoing disciplinary and social conversation. This can occur with any material that students assume to be true: whether in the fields of economics, psychology, management, agricultural policy, or engineering. "What do they think they know and why do they think they know it?" is the first question that we must ask on the first day of every semester. While where we go from there will be heavily dependent upon our individual disciplines, that question remains key to our own work as knowledgeable, responsible, and creative undergraduate teachers.

In fact, it is a knowledge base that I must establish immediately in order to know how best to meet the needs of a given class and one that I rarely have difficulty in determining. Unlike Graff, I have found that Johnny (or Susie, Graff's other fictional student) enjoys speaking out, or beginning to converse, on controversial, cherished, or vocationally relevant topics—and almost always does so with little prompting—but what does concern me is the content of what Johnny and Susie say and the presuppositions underlying their assertions. This pedagogical shift from simply generating conversational activity to focusing on conversational content allows me to supplement and continue the conversation that Graff himself has usefully initiated.

As an example: in his eighth chapter, "Why Johnny Can't Argue," Graff makes a compelling case for the necessity of focusing on argumentation in teaching students how to write, think, and academically empower themselves. He offers argument "templates" (developed by Cathy Birkenstein) that direct students to respond to a text with their forthright assertion of agreement or disagreement, and then to follow that assertion with evidence. He concludes the chapter with the observation, "Johnny and Susie are often forceful arguers out of school, and they can be forceful arguers in school if the moves of the game are not kept from them" (172). He later urges students to "[b]egin your text by directly identifying the prior conversation or debate that you are entering" and "[m]ake a claim, the sooner the better, preferably flagged for the reader by a phrase like 'My claim here is that . . . ' " (275). Prompting students into such a declaration certainly has a use value in getting their opinions out in the open, but in my experience, students make such declarations easily and often already, especially compared to some of the European students whom I mentioned earlier.

The real challenge I have faced over my many years in higher education is that in a heterogeneous student group, the claim or argument could very well be that "All southerners are poorly educated and racist, and here are some examples that support my views." Or "Homosexuals are an abomination and I have passages from Leviticus to prove it." The most important question facing the educator is, then, "Where do I go from there?" In trying to adapt Graff's work for my own pedagogical use, I find that the problem is not that students can't or don't argue, it is that they argue with an often rigid basis in traditional or stereotypical notions and largely uninterrogated belief systems. They are often quite willing to add to an ongoing conversation, but without knowledge, responsibility, and innovation.

Graff asks students to consider first, "What conversation are you in?" (157), adding that "when student writing is flat and unfocused, the reason often lies in a failure to provide students with a conversation to argue *in*" (157). He continues, "[I]f we can let students in on the secret that intellectual writing and discussion are extensions of their normal conversation practices, much of the mystification can be dissipated and the struggling students have a shot at catching up" (158). I largely agree, but I would add that what we must do more explicitly in higher education generally, just as we do already in much of our own academic writing, is engage in a conversation *about* hasty judgments and problematic arguments based in prejudice and formulaic thinking. That is the conversation they are entering, not a conversation that might be reducible to: "Are homosexuals an abomination, yes or no?"

Graff does not mention the work of Gadamer, but there are some interesting ways that Gadamer and some of his interlocutors help us as teachers of undergraduates (and potential "specific intellectuals") make use of Graff's emphasis on assertion, conversation, and argumentation within the classroom. "Prejudice"—or prejudgment—must be the target of our, and our students', skillfully conducted analysis and argumentation. Knowledge, responsibility, and innovation all derive from a critical engagement with prejudgment.

In *Truth and Method*, Gadamer famously recuperates the power and even mundane necessity of *Vorurteil*, which can be translated from the German as either "prejudice" or prejudgment. This recuperation has led to some misunderstandings of (what we might even call prejudicial dismissals of) Gadamer and his relevance to progressive thinking and pedagogy. In spite of these few hasty readings by critics, Gadamer never celebrates prejudice or traditional thinking in a thoughtless or reactionary way. Instead, he notes that prejudgments are the bases of daily life and for all movement toward broader understanding. In fact, and as his biographer Jean Grondin argues, "All understanding is always only a project, only provisional" (*Philosophy*, 75), and those provisional judgments metamorphose as we continue our endless quest for understanding. At the same time, we could not exist in the complexity of a single day's requirements for decision making if we did not rest comfortably on some prejudgments that we never interrogate: if I run that red light, I will injure myself and others; if I am consistently late to work, I will be reprimanded or fired; if I fail to pay my rent, I will be evicted. As I noted in my recent book *Queer Theories*, even living "queerly" is not living in a state of chaos. We must respond formulaically in most situations, and that is equally true for the most radical or conservative among us.

However, from Gadamer, Ricoeur, and Foucault, we learn that an energetic critical engagement with some prejudgments and traditions is exactly what living as an intellectual should mean. Even if we must exist in a constant state of prejudice, our critical task is to sort out which prejudgments are necessary or relatively benign, and which are destructive, oppressive, and untenable. Gadamer observes that "there is undoubtedly no understanding that is free of all prejudices, however much the will of our knowledge must be directed toward escaping their thrall" (*Truth and Method*, 490). The importance of that quest for critical distinction and knowledge is his central concern in *Truth and Method*: "What distinguishes legitimate prejudices from the countless others which it is the undeniable task of critical reason to overcome?" (277). Gadamer's question points us to the most important overall thrust for student analysis and argumentation as well: isolating, accounting for, and critiquing the prejudgments and traditions that comprise the knowledge base in their academic and vocational fields, and their everyday lives. That common project of argumentation about prejudice and inevitably changing notions of what is "true" can link the projects of Graffian pedagogy, Gadamerian philosophical hermeneutics, and Foucauldian specific intellectualism.

Indeed, for feminist educators working with Gadamerian philosophical hermeneutics, these linkages have developed considerable appeal. They highlight the power and necessity of social conventions without assuming that they are unalterable, and focus on conversation as a key component of any process of alteration. The philosopher Lorraine Code writes, "Interpretive understanding begins when someone/something addresses us and we attempt to respond. It requires a suspension of our prejudices in the sense of putting them into question, opening up and keeping open other possibilities while taking account of its own (i.e. interpretation's own) historicality" (*Feminist Interpretations*, 9). Georgia Warnke further relates this Gadamerian insight to her work as a scholar, teacher, and activist: "Gender is an interpretation, a fusion between the wants and needs of developing individuals and the history of interpretations of them, including objections to those interpretations. . . . To some extent [Gadamer's] analysis buttresses [Judith] Butler's. . . . [Our gender identities are] the interpreted fusions that we currently are. At the same time, we can acknowledge their interpretive character and modify them if we think we should" ("Hermeneutics and Constructed Identities," 72). This is not instrumentality whereby we change our "selves" with mechanical ease; it is an always slippery process by which we reference an ideal of significant change but return to work on the particulars of the lived and necessarily, incrementally metamorphic.

Susan Hekman discusses Gadamer's potential utility for feminists in ways useful for all of us working in higher education today. She contends that "Gadamer's emphasis on tradition offers feminism an opportunity to explore its greatest contemporary challenge: how to effect change within the existing set of meanings that constitute society" ("Ontology of Change," 184). Hekman goes on to note that Gadamer supplements Foucault in practical and important ways: "Foucault claims that there are gaps and silences between discourses; subjugated knowledges can rise to the surface, breaking the hegemony of established discourses of knowledge. But exactly how this occurs is not specified" (191). Gadamer fills in that blank: "Every experience, he claims, is a confrontation—it sets something new against sometime old. . . . The disruption of a new experience, in particular, can reveal a previous opinion to be untenable. . . . The constant juxtaposition of tradition and new experiences, understood in the context of the historical situatedness of all understanding, provides Gadamer's hermeneutics with its critical possibility" (193). That is not to say that a new situation or new information might not simply be recuperated within old paradigms or dismissed out of hand, but the potential in the classroom and in intellectual work generally is to bring the confrontation between old and new, tradition and revision, to a point of consciousness and overt expression.

And this is the *potential*, at least, for the argumentative process that Graff highlights as necessary to student skill-building and empowerment. In fact, I see it as key to our mission as educators to "raise consciousness" in our classrooms, however old-fashioned that phrase might seem. In some fields, that consciousness-raising may mean approaching textbook material and current disciplinary "truths" as ones that will inevitably be revised and sparking student interest in contributing to that metamorphosis. In my cultural studies classes, and as an educator trained in Paolo Freire and Foucault and feminist theorists from the past half century, my specific intellectual work is to help students better critique their own cultural positions. Again, Graff provides some very useful starting points. His epilogue reminds students to "Enter a conversation just as you do in real life," "Make a claim," and "Remind readers of your claim" (275). Yet if Graff's injunctions are going to have continuing relevance to the work we do beyond composition classes populated by particularly inert students, they have to be bracketed with an insistence on some critical attachment to the presuppositions or traditions behind the conversation that they are entering. "Real life" and its argumentative frames of reference are *the problem* from a Gadamerian and Foucauldian intellectual perspective. As intellectuals in training, students should learn *not* to enter disciplinary and consequential social conversations as they might argue over a bar tab or poker hand; they should attempt first to understand the terms of the conversation and the norms encoded therein. Then they should enter the conversation and advance a thesis. That constitutes an intellectualism based in knowledge, responsibility, and innovation. If those emphases mean that students learn to hesitate before advancing an argument, that is for the good. Rushing into assertions often means a stunning lack of reflection on the impact or consequences of a proposed agenda. Action without sufficient thought is already too common in the current American social and political scene.

Graff writes, "I would make the case for the pedagogical value even of 'crude' debate, if only as a precondition of advancing subsequently to more nuanced, less reductively polarized conversations" (*Clueless in Academe*, 94). I have a different perspective. I do not believe that we should ever start from crude debate, even if we value an energetic exchange of opinions and analysis. For two people to start by shouting crudely "You're an abomination" and "You're a breeder" (or "You're a liberal" and "You're a fundie") is not a healthy precondition to anything. In my own pedagogical and life experiences, I have never found that crude attacks on beliefs or identity positions, which Graff would seem to countenance in the quotation above, lead regularly to nuanced conversations. Even in eliciting from students their base of knowledge or opinion, as I do in every class, I urge them always to keep statements in the first person. Conversation and nuanced interaction grow from emerging and deepening reflections upon those "I" statements.

Gadamer again helps us refine some of Graff's concepts: "To be in a conversation . . . means to be beyond oneself, to think with the other, and to come back to oneself as if to another" ("Destrucktion *and Deconstruction*," 110). That cannot happen without a metareflective move and some critical awareness of the presuppositions behind our own and others' cherished beliefs. Crudeness does not allow that, or, in fact, it is not crudeness. Gadamer admits that "one can never by means of reflection place oneself in an externalized relation to one's situation" (*Gadamer in Conversation*, 46), but such externalization can be achieved, even if always imperfectly, through conversation itself. What matters then, for my pedagogical purposes, are the conditions under which productive conversation can occur with the goal of such enlarged and transformed perspectives. At the very least, this potentially radical conversational engagement demands a willingness to put one's own opinions at risk, and that decision must precede the decision to assert. That is a key aspect of "responsibility" as it links knowledge (or what we think we know) and innovation (or what we would like to see in the future).

Given the growing popularity of freshman seminars, and other university or college life introductory forums, we are already developing venues where the necessity to risk and reevaluate, as part of an intellectually responsible life, can first be articulated as central to an undergraduate education. In fact, the extent to which students have risked and reevaluated their beliefs over the course of their education is something that we must find ways of measuring in exit assessments. This does not involve a process of ideological indoctrination, and it does not revolve around a set of positions that students are expected to parrot back to us. It is, instead, a set of necessary life skills that have clear and explainable vocational, as well as communal, value. These are the skills of innovative thinking, life-long learning, and continuing critical investigation. They help undercut doctrinal thinking on both the left end and the right end of the political spectrum, in inculcating the core principles of openness to others and to the inevitability and desirability of change.

Yet most of the readers of this book may have little immediate ability to influence the goals of freshman seminars or the broad definitions of a university's mission. When we do have leverage, however, it is important to make our perspectives on intellectualism and the desired outcomes of a university education known. Of course, we must continue to seek out new opportunities to exercise such influence. Indeed, those who complain most bitterly about the "state of the institution" where they are employed are often the ones least likely to involve themselves in the service opportunities that would contribute to their institution's improvement—faculty governance bodies, planning committees, core (or general education) curriculum committees, and assessment bodies. Here as elsewhere, if we don't like aspects of our institution, it is *our* responsibility to address them as opportunities present themselves. That is *our* specific intellectual work.

But even more to the point, our work in this arena must start in all of the venues that we do find at hand. Even as we ensure that we understand the guidelines and goals of our college or university, so that our work reinforces that of our colleagues, we can also adapt our classroom policies and practices to emphasize the practical, real-life intellectualism that I have been discussing here. It means asking students in every one of our classes to understand the content of the conversation that comprises the field of study at hand, and then to add responsibly and thoughtfully to that conversation with their own innovative work and thoughtful opinions. It means shifting the desired outcomes of our pedagogies from "mastery" of course material to "dialogic interaction" with that material (which always requires a depth of understanding and does not, therefore, abandon the expectation of knowledge underlying the rhetoric of "mastery"). For my part, I make intellectual risk-taking the explicitly identified mode of operation of all of my classes. Even for the most pragmatic of students, I can explain it successfully as a quality of mind that will keep them employed in a rapidly changing world and allow them to succeed in personal and professional arenas where innovation is almost always rewarded over inertia and inflexibility. To put it into the bluntest terms for them, people lose their jobs every day because they cannot innovate and acquire new perspectives on old knowledge bases. The skills that they learn at university, even in theory-based cultural studies classes, are ones that do have a practical payoff. It is always incumbent upon me as the instructor to clearly articulate that payoff to them.

To focus on specifics here, my emphasis on students learning to "shift" perspective leads to classroom exercises and projects in which I, like Graff, ask them to challenge the texts they read. Graff's most recent work, *They Say/I Say: The Moves That Matter in Academic Writing* (co-written with Cathy Birkenstein), is a textbook based on *Clueless in Academe* that contains some excellent exercises encouraging students to structure their academic writing around moves that mirror the entering of a literal conversation (as the title suggests). These are useful in a wide variety of writing-based courses and argumentative contexts. Furthermore, out-of-class writing exercises or in-class group projects in which students summarize the argument of a writer, theorist, or other interlocutor, and then clearly articulate their response (full agreement and why, partial agreement and why, or substantial disagreement and why) allows us immediately to establish the base of opinion that will lead to productive classroom exchange. Indeed, these are "life moves" in that students will have to make similar arguments in their work lives and personal lives long after they exit the university.

However, as I have been suggesting throughout this chapter, the university experience is not only about learning to marshal evidence effectively. It is also about probing one's own opinions, listening to counterarguments, and learning to shift perspective. My substantial gloss on *Clueless in Academe* and *They Say/I Say* is in maintaining that students need to have their entrenched opinions interrogated and unsettled in every class they take, and they need to be reminded that an intellectual and successful professional life means changing one's mind, not simply finding clever ways to justify one's initial assertions. Therefore, I often ask students to play a devil's advocacy role, to test the logic of their own presuppositions and to marshal evidence to support positions that they may not fully understand or even agree with. This allows them at least to begin to see the world through someone else's eyes, to discover where entrenched disagreement comes from, and to start to understand when and why it may be necessary to compromise on opinions that they may have forcefully asserted in the past.

In writing projects, in classroom discussions, and in life generally, they do enter conversations, as Graff notes, but they also must learn to probe the premises underlying individual perspectives, including their own. If they do not, as I explain carefully to them, they will always be at loggerheads with others, and this is an intransigence that will have dire vocational and social consequences. To this end, I often ask them to trace the genesis of their beliefs, to write brief essays outlining what aspects of their perspectives on a given subject are tenaciously held and what aspects are ones on which they might compromise, and to probe how their beliefs reflect a certain, always circumscribed, positioning in the world (of class, gender, geographical location). For a few, there is no possibility of compromise on a given issue; there is simply "nothing to discuss" on a subject fundamental to their belief system. Indeed, I, too, have certain opinions that I hold very tenaciously. But in discussing those beliefs as reflecting a personal history, a temporal and cultural location, and a set of foundational premises, they and I can at least come to an understanding of why others may hold very different opinions with equal tenacity. That understanding fosters dialogue, even if compromise may be elusive or impossible on some issues. Certainly I don't convince all of my students of the worth of intellectual risk-taking as a way of life, but I do engage enough in a process of critical self-reflection to create a general environment conducive to intellectual growth and exchange.

In "The Tasks of the Political Educator," Ricoeur writes, "I believe, in fact, that there is a historic function of utopia in the social order. Only utopia can give to economic, social, and political action a human intention and, in my sense, a double intention: on the one hand the will of humanity as a totality; on the other hand, the will of the person as a singularity" (289). All students should be able to articulate that vision for a better future, whatever their cherished beliefs. Indeed, nothing that I say above is meant to imply that students should not hold and retain very diverse perspectives on the world and what that utopia entails. So what if, you might ask, a student's "utopia" involves patently racist, sexist, anti-Semitic, or homophobic aspects? I have no easy answer to that question, but firmly believe that it is far better for those beliefs to be expressed and held up to conversational scrutiny than it is for them to remain unarticulated and unscrutinized. It is not my job, even as a cultural studies professor, to disallow or censor positions that I find personally troubling. It is my job, however, to get students to marshal evidence to support their opinions and to require them to critique thoroughly the basis for the views that they bring to the subjects at hand. That is the intellectualism that I am calling for here, and that is also a form of continuing self-reflection that is still sorely needed in general public discourse in this country. In fact, that hermeneutic dynamic of self-reflection in the context of energetic conversation *constitutes* my vision of an ideal future.

And on that point I actually find some conversational common ground with David Horowitz and the politicians who are supporting his so-called Academic Bill of Rights. Vigorous, perspective-expanding conversation demands a diversity of viewpoints, including conservative, middle-of-the-road, and leftist. The most uninteresting classes I ever took as a student and have taught as a professor are those in which everyone agrees on everything. Frankly I have never had a close colleague who thought otherwise. Thus where I clearly part ways with Horowitz is in his oft-leveled charges of rampant discrimination against conservative students; I have simply never seen that happen. Everyone's viewpoints should be challenged and changed in the experience of higher education. Nothing makes me feel like more of a success in my role as classroom conversation facilitator than the e-mails I get from students—conservative and liberal, American and European—who say that they remember my class as a place where they were able to complicate their understanding of issues and knowledge areas that they thought they knew well, but that they are now continuing to reflect upon, sometimes years afterwards, as they work toward even greater understanding.

And, of course, the risk-taking that I discuss here must include the instructor as well. In a room full of Johnnies and Susies, many will possess knowledge that we lack, and one thing that Graff does superbly is to remind all educators that students bring to the classroom their own expertise. We should never forget that many of our students will have experience bases that make their engagement with the subject matter at hand far different from ours, especially when we pay attention to generation, as well as gender, race, and class positioning. This provides particularly exciting base matter upon which conversation can draw. Graff takes seriously the work of Thomas McLaughlin in *Street Smarts and Critical Theory*, a book that I, too, find useful, and he reminds educators to attend to student's nascent critical skills in responding to each other and to popular culture, out of their own identity political affiliations. I would add that because of this base of student expertise, the undergraduate educator must also be an enthusiastic learner, because she or he must always first acknowledge what students can also teach us about their backgrounds and analytical engagements. As a forty-six-year-old university professor who has spent most of his adult life in urban areas, I still have a lot to learn about the lives and perspectives of my West Virginian students, many of whom are in their twenties and have solid skills, certainly different from mine, at negotiating lives on the margins of small Appalachian towns. If I am going to "add value" to those skills, first I have to educate myself about what they already know and do well.

In ways pertinent to our discussion here, bell hooks, in *Teaching to Transgress*, speaks of the importance of personal narratives in the classroom: "Engaged pedagogy necessarily values student expression. . . . When education is the practice of freedom, students are not the only ones who are asked to share, to confess. . . . When professors bring narratives of their own experiences into classroom discussions it eliminates the possibility that we can function as all-knowing, silent interrogators" (20–21). It is imperative that we, in the process of mentoring our students into intellectualism, also demystify our own work and intellectualism. Unless we reveal to students that an intellectual life is also a human, fragile, and imperfect life, it will always seem impossible, impractical, or simply dishonest.

How precisely we exchange those narratives will obviously depend upon the individual class and its format. But if a reflective, practical intellectualism is an ongoing goal of undergraduate education, those narratives will emerge and reemerge in numerous class settings. If students are expected as part of their first-year experience to articulate their values and vision for their lives—their life plans—then the narrating of the "self" becomes a part of their understanding of what happens at a university. Individual classes then open without anxiety with forthright statements of how a given class will draw on students' previous knowledge and how it dovetails (or perhaps, in their opinion, does not dovetail) with those life plans as narratives always under revision. For the educator also to bring in her or his own life plan, goals, vision, and values in a classroom is to make more transparent the role she or he will play in the dialogic process that is successful teaching. I start every course with a session in which students talk about their own previous experiences with related materials, their hopes and fears regarding the course, and how it fits into their academic course of study or life plan. Then I do the same.

The purpose of such exercises is more than simply breaking the ice or finding out what expectations students bring to a particular class (so that my expectations can be adjusted accordingly), it also furthers a process of life goal establishment and revision in a context of the pursuit of knowledge, responsibility, and innovation. The cumulative effect of numerous encounters with such exercises and in a variety of classes is, I hope, a honed ability to place one's own life in dialogue with others, to approach "authorities" as individuals with their own lives and failings, and to textualize a set of values and commitments that can be justified in communal conversation (and with the ability also to address sensitively the values and commitments of others). Indeed, that simple but elusive outcome of learning to add to conversations knowledgeably, responsibly, and creatively is a compelling justification for a university education that we can all articulate, over and above any static knowledge base that could be acquired from CDs, DVDs, and self-study guides available from online suppliers. Supple conversational skills are life skills and vocational skills, as well as social survival skills, indeed, those needed for our world to survive. These are the core components of an intellectualism that is integrated into life.

One of Graff's most memorable injunctions directed at academics primarily, but with use value for students, too, is "Dare to Be Reductive" (*Clueless in Academe*, 136); in other words, don't be afraid to put things in their simplest or most accessible terms. I would agree generally. But as a queer individual, I have certainly been the target over my lifetime of a lot of verbal and even physical violence that derives from reductive notions of who and what I am. Being reductive and hasty in reductive assertions is already a significant problem in American life. I at least want us to remember that an acknowledgment of the reductive as reductive is actually the beginning of a very long and exciting conversation. It is the beginning of an intellectual life and the beginning of a sense of passion toward and commitment to a vocation and set of life goals and purposes. The opportunity afforded to us in undergraduate education is to help students to acquire the knowledge and sense of responsibility necessary to innovate within the conversations that precede and include them. In doing so, they and we can transform the world in thoughtful ways.

chapter three

· · · · · · · · · · · · ·

Changing Graduate
Education

*i*N THE SUMMER of 2005, I had what was probably a once-in-a-lifetime opportunity, indeed, one that very few writers are ever afforded. I discovered, by chance, a blog that had just been created by a group of students and faculty who were about to begin reading and discussing my book *The Academic Self: An Owner's Manual.* I followed their commentary as it was posted and found the entire experience of overhearing the unfiltered responses of two dozen or so readers at once incredibly intimate, somewhat unsettling, and extraordinarily illuminating. Of course, I had read reviews of my books before, including *The Academic Self,* but they were usually delicately expressed and carefully edited, and certainly were temporally separated from the actual reading experience. Few of us ever get to experience our readers' reactions, more or less, as they are reading. I never revealed to the bloggers that I was listening in, and no matter how much I wanted to say, "No, no, that is not what I meant at all . . ." I simply let the discussion continue as it should, without an overprotective author there to jump in and defend his assumptions or assertions.

But one comment has stuck with me because it revealed just how much things have changed and are continuing to change on some of the issues that the present book also addresses. On June 10, one blogger ("Tiruncula") posted the following comment and questions:

62

Hall complains early on that the 4–4 loads that come with many available jobs "were never even mentioned" by grad school professors. While I take his point that grad school professors implicitly or explicitly train their students to replicate their own research careers and that grad school typically offers little direct preparation for teaching-intensive jobs, I'm flummoxed by the notion that one could get all the way to the job-search stage of a PhD and have no idea what was out there waiting. Did Hall pay no attention at all to the job searches of those a few years ahead of him in his program? Did he have no contact with alumni of his program? Were his interactions with professors limited to those old and sheltered enough not to have passed through less glamorous jobs on the way to the the [sic] exalted positions in which they were privileged to teach the (no doubt extremely irritating, if highly self-motivated) Mr. Hall? (Sorry, I'm getting a little crabby here.)

(http://academicself.blogspot.com/2005_06_01_academicself_archive.
html)

In retrospect, I probably was extremely irritating to some of my professors, but the larger concern expressed here is that there were professional development opportunities that were available and that I (and many others, too) simply ignored.

That was not the case, and demonstrates thankfully how far we as a profession have come in just a few years. In 1989 and 1990 there were no professional development talks, panels, or visits by alumni. Any discussion of jobs that entailed a 4–4 course load was muted or nervously avoided because the University of Maryland, at that time, was interested in raising its profile nationally and certainly did not want to be perceived as a feeder program to teaching schools. One of my mentors (and the job placement advisor during my two searches) wrote later in a dialogue we published on graduate education that she had always seen herself as "preparing students for a very narrow band of jobs, from the equivalent of my own at a large research university to posts in four-year liberal arts colleges or branches of state universities, preferably not in departments with four-course-per-semester teaching loads unless the student clearly doesn't want to do writing or research" ("That Was Then, This Is Now," 214). Those teaching in the graduate program at the University of Maryland who had actually moved up through the ranks, so to speak, of "less glamorous" jobs—and I know now there was at least one—never discussed that history with those of us on the market; if their silence was attributable to shame or simple lack of concern for us is something that I will never know. But, frankly, very few members of the faculty spoke to us about their careers. Others and I certainly were self-motivated in many ways, but questions about the wide variety of jobs out there as possibilities never occurred to any of us. The writer above goes on to say in the same posting that I seem to have moved through my PhD program in "a very blinkered way," but truthfully many of us were blinkered in 1990. I'm certainly not blaming the (mostly very) good folks at the University of Maryland for any of the above; it was simply a different time and a different mind-set that has largely been supplanted. Inside of one paradigm today, it is hard to imagine that another was operant just a few years ago.

As is no doubt clear by now, I believe that the rise of professional studies and professional development in PhD programs over the past two decades have been very positive things generally. Yes, it means that student anxiety levels have increased in some ways; graduate students no longer simply worry about acquiring knowledge and planning a dissertation, but also about giving conference papers, publishing, and otherwise building a vita. But by encountering those stressors now, students are much better informed about the stress that they will encounter for the rest of the careers they are contemplating. Through programs that do inform students now about the range of career paths possible in and outside of the academy, we are doing a much better job generally at recognizing our students' needs and the realities of their future work lives. After all, the vast majority of students exiting the PhD program at the University of Maryland in the early 1990s entered jobs exactly like the one I found, at regional comprehensive universities or small colleges with teaching, not research, missions. I would say that we in graduate education, and students exiting our graduate programs, are far less "blinkered" today than was the case just a few years ago.

I can attest to that firsthand and from a couple of different angles. Chairing hiring committees at a teaching-centered university (Cal State Northridge) for almost a decade (1995–2004) and interviewing hundreds of candidates for the twenty or so new positions that I hired for, I saw a dramatic shift in candidates' abilities to discuss their priorities and a new depth to their understanding of careers at teaching schools. Over the years, they have generally become far less likely to expect careers exactly like those of their graduate school mentors. Now that I teach in a doctoral program preparing students for possible careers in the academy, I see how different the discussion and training are compared to what I encountered. Alumni do return to talk about their jobs to aspiring academics, and we on the faculty often speak with students about our careers with the vagaries, joys, and disappointments on relatively full display. I believe that we have largely demythologized the position of "professor," especially compared to the heyday of the academic "star" in the 1980s when certain privileged academics were treated like, and often believed themselves to be, beings worthy of near-religious worship. Thankfully, that is no longer the case. As Geoffrey Galt Harpham, who ran Tulane's Program in Literary Theory during the star system's height, has remarked, "[W]hat we now call the 'profession' is not generating stars, so that yesterday's stars remain today's, but older and fatter and generally less stellar than they used to be" ("End of Theory," 193). If the process of "professionalization" killed the star system, as Harpham elsewhere in the same essay implies, then that is yet another reason to be thankful for it. For all academics to be seen as human rather than otherworldly is better for students and the professorate alike. No one benefits from a system that encourages even more inflated egos among a group that already has a tendency to think of itself as much smarter than the general population.

Nevertheless, I still think that there are ways that we can continue fine-tuning our processes and goals in graduate education. Reading job applications and conducting interviews provide a venue for a form of outcomes assessment, and having been involved now in about two dozen hiring processes in the past decade, I applaud our successes but also want to point to some opportunities that present themselves still. Through their processes of professional development, our graduate programs today are usually creating researchers and writers who know—or are clearly learn-ing—how to disseminate their work in print and conference presentation, teachers who are increasingly up to the challenge of educating diversely skilled groups of undergraduates and integrating new technologies into their classrooms, and thinkers who are beginning to see their careers as ones not tied to a simple or fixed narrative of what constitutes "success" in the academy. These are strengths that we can build upon because several challenges remain.

Indeed, one useful way to refine even further our expectations for graduate training is a version of what I proposed in my last chapter on undergraduate education. While our expectations for graduate-level work are certainly different from and more rigorous than they are in the undergraduate classroom, we are training in both venues well-informed and highly skilled participants in the conversations that comprise their fields of study. In both venues it is also important to emphasize that to be a responsible participant in a conversation is, in effect, to be a responsible member of a community or set of communities. Indeed, for those graduate students training for an academic career, it is vital for them to recognize that certain communal/conversational dynamics *and* responsibilities link the work that academics do in the classroom, in their scholarly fields, and in their institutions. It is that last aspect of our work lives in the academy that deserves even greater attention in the professional development process. We have developed excellent teaching and research workshops and manuals for our graduate students; however, service and other collegial interactions and activities are major professional responsibilities that still receive far too little notice in our conversations with aspiring academics.

This is where the interview as "outcomes assessment venue" offers useful data. Out of the hundreds of interviews I've conducted, only a handful of applicants have been able to muster an answer to a question on the type of service that would interest them, beyond a vague, "Oh, I'm happy to do some." Even fewer have talked about service as a welcome component of their projected careers, even with considerable prompting on my part. Of course, more training in service and other forms of collegial interaction is occurring in graduate programs now than was the case a generation ago. It is much more common today for students to sit on major department committees, including some hiring committees, and for students themselves to put on conferences and other events that require committee work and hours working collegially with other students and faculty members. But, still, little is written or said about institutional citizenship as a concept and set of activities that is connected intellectually and intimately to the other work that we do. We on the faculty rarely discuss it among ourselves and even more rarely broach the topic with students.

We might clarify our terms here by recognizing that "service" as a professional practice is the placement of communal needs above our own narrow interests and desires. Whether manifested in department committee work, in the mentoring of junior colleagues, in work on program oversight bodies, in participation in senates or assemblies, or in activity as readers, evaluators, or public educators, it requires a deflation of the individual ego in the service of broad social rather than narrowly self-interested values. In a sense, it represents the opposite of the bloated self-regard of the "star" or "diva," because it demands humility, a sacrifice of time and energy that could be used instead for careerist purposes, and an ability to reach consensus, or at least agree to disagree, and then to move forward with a group process. If, as Harpham maintains, professionalization killed the star system, then a deepening emphasis on service as a valuable and necessary component of our professional lives can put the final nail in its coffin.

Indeed, a productive emphasis on service as institutional citizenship allows us to address with students a topic that is often wholly avoided when discussing academic careers: collegiality. It is worth remembering, of course, that collegiality as an issue in tenure and promotion cases was long abused by retrograde forces in the academy—it was deployed to deny tenure to women, people of color, individuals working in identity political fields, and those who resisted harassment or attempted to change a culture of abuse. Sometimes it was referenced with less explicitly nefarious intent but with the same consequences, when departments simply did not understand the shifts that were occurring in the broader academy and reacted with incomprehension to still untenured agents of change within their own institutions.

I am certainly *not* advocating a return to the use of "collegiality" as a murky and highly subjective assessment field in tenure reviews. Personnel processes should always rest upon clearly documented and verifiable evidence, and collegiality rarely provides that except in the most egregious instances of its absence. However, I do think collegial behavior is necessary for the effective functioning of an academic community, is a subject worth discussing (especially during mentoring sessions) with those individuals newly joining a given community, and is also a topic we must address with graduate students aspiring to reach that stage. Collegiality means responsible citizenship within our institutions, embracing the same qualities that one would hope for in responsible citizens of the nation and globe: thoughtfulness, attentiveness to the needs of others, and a willingness to listen carefully and engage in meaningful communication across and in spite of differences. It means an ability to work collaboratively to solve problems and set priorities, and, finally, it means a commitment to the ethical treatment of others, and especially those in disempowered positions (such as staff members, part-timers, and junior faculty, in an academic context). All of this may sound like a no-brainer to some graduate student readers of this book, but we who work in large and diverse departments know how often collegiality breaks down or is threatened by the dysfunctional among us, including those with tendencies toward cynicism, egomania, and paranoia.

In fact, I am sure I am not alone in knowing competent teachers who publish prolifically, but who also act abusively toward staff members and colleagues (to the point of ridiculing, yelling, and sometimes even making thinly disguised threats). I have always been stunned when people have defended such egomaniacal or "diva"-like behavior, inside or outside the academy. No amount of talent or "genius" gives one the right to treat one's fellow department citizens as objects of scorn or as pin cushions for abuse. As many of us know well, those egomaniacs are as just common among groups of radical queers, feminists, and Marxists as they are among the "old boys" who used to control all sectors of the academy. Frankly, I do not care how famous someone is or how fabulous his or her research may be, an egomaniac should not be a member of a department community in an educational institution if she or he refuses to treat staff and colleagues with respect. While such extreme problems are outside of the scope of this discussion, certainly it is always a core job responsibility of administrators to document carefully and address forthrightly any abusive workplace behavior. In most institutions, verifiable evidence of abuse already is, and certainly always should be, considered gravely as a part of any promotion, tenure, or posttenure review.

But the question remains here, how do we frame the professionalization of graduate students to help mitigate potential problems by embracing fully all of the areas of professional responsibility catalogued above: teaching, research, service, and collegiality? An emphasis on conversation and the ability to participate productively and humbly in dialogue can provide that frame and an overall strategy for the mentoring and development of new professionals. Successful teaching demands an ability to engage productively in classroom conversations. Responsible scholarship and research develops from a knowledgeable and productive conversation with one's predecessors and peers in a field of inquiry. Effective service on committees and in the public sphere demands an openness to the ideas of others and an ability to respond to those ideas with skill and self-awareness. Finally, collegiality draws daily on a commitment to productive and responsible communication.

Indeed, the overarching point of this book is that if we are going to be agents of change within our departments, institutions, research fields, and broader communities, we have to be able to engage in caring and careful dialogue, embracing the possibilities of an intellectualism that is professionally self-aware and eager to engage others in potentially transformative exchange. It is worth reiterating, these are not feel-good, chicken-soup-for-the-soul musings and suggestions; they are ones fully supported by some of the most significant work in contemporary philosophy and research on subjectivity and social change. Hans Herbert Kögler, in a provocative book titled *The Power of Dialogue*, suggests that by synthesizing Gadamerian conversation and Foucauldian specific intellectualism and situated knowledge, we can construct a paradigm of intellectual work "in which the reflexive self becomes aware of its origins and *thereby* becomes the possible source of new identities" (275). This shift demands a conversational dynamic, because "the perspective from the other's point of view . . . sheds a specific light on ourselves that we could not have generated by ourselves" (252). The result of this emphasis on the "reflexively critical self" is an ongoing "ethical practice . . . in which respect for the other as well as a furthering of possible forms of self-realization are reconciled" (275). This transformative, conversational process really rests on a few basic principles: we listen carefully to others, allow their perspectives to denaturalize our own assumptions, engage with enthusiasm in explanations of our own lives and perspectives, and learn to work within that process of dialogue toward understanding, mutual tolerance of abiding differences, and social and political structures that allow for and even value such differences (a process that captures well the dynamic of "listening rhetoric" described by the late Wayne C. Booth in his last major work, *The Rhetoric of Rhetoric*). Yet as relatively simple as this might appear on the surface, especially, one might think, for skilled academics, it is surprising how often conversations and collegiality break down in department meetings, committees, and hallway interactions.

In fact, a Gadamerian emphasis on openness, humility, and an overarching commitment to engaging in dialogue helps address some concerns expressed by previous commentators on academic professional training and graduate education. In the mid-1990s, David Damrosch worried that "[w]e scholars rightly cherish our independence of mind and our originality of perspective, but we need to balance the hermeneutics of exile with a more creative hermeneutics of community" (*We Scholars*, 213). His suggestions for greater collaboration among graduate students and an opening up of possibilities for new dissertation models remain timely and useful. Similarly, Bill Readings in the posthumously published, and still justly famous, *The University in Ruins* called for a new paradigm for education: "[T]o think beside each other and beside ourselves, is to explore an open network of obligations that keeps the question of meaning open as a locus of debate" (165). This is education that values the training of both students and professors in the ability to speak with an audience that "is not [simply] a general public; it is an agglomeration of people of widely differing ages, classes, genders, sexualities, ethnicities, and so on" (165). More recently, Frank H. T. Rhodes worries that PhD training does little "to meet the fundamental needs and address the larger issues of contemporary society . . . ; to foster research only coincidentally promotes citizenship that addresses the needs of society. To develop skills in some exquisitely refined area of research may contribute little to the large-minded view of knowledge that a university teacher should exemplify" (*Creation of the Future*, 124). To refine our goals in processes of graduate training and especially professional development to embrace engaged and self-reflective conversation helps mitigate the destructive force of what Damrosch terms the "myth" and too often "reality" "of the scholar as isolated individual" (*We Scholars*, 188).

Yet even as commentators have for years called for changes in graduate education, there have been few specifics. Tweaking the design of the dissertation or calling vaguely for civic-mindedness hardly helps a graduate director who is interested in rethinking her program or a faculty member who wants to begin a discussion or make concrete recommendations to a department on how better to meet the needs of graduate students. I offer some of my own suggestions below and also know that many of my readers could offer many "best practices" that are not yet programmatically validated. These need to be aired in conversations within programs.

Indeed, every graduate program—whether granting the MA, MFA, clinical, or doctoral degree—should engage in such conversations to define precisely its goals and expectations, and I believe these should always embrace explicitly how best to provide student training in institutional and broader forms of citizenship. This does happen already, but it can be even more clearly emphasized in several different arenas:

In Graduate Classes and Seminars

After seven years as a graduate student and then another sixteen teaching in graduate programs, I have some very decided opinions about what should and should not occur in graduate classes. The most stressful and (in retrospect) useless courses that I took as a grad student were ones that pitted student against student in forms of antagonistic and hypercompetitive gamesmanship. To be sure, some of us were able to compete adroitly in such an environment; after all, graduate students are usually quick-witted and driven to succeed, otherwise they wouldn't have made it, or even wanted to make it, as far as graduate school. Some of us were quite able to marshal a caustic comment, point out a flaw with deadly accuracy, and try always to make the smartest comment in class and thereby effectively keep center stage—*if* the professor demanded and rewarded such behavior. I remember one young professor who loved to see seminar participants humiliated by classmates eager to rip apart an argument and shred an ego. No doubt he had participated in the same dynamic in his own (then still recent) graduate school experience. This is the model of the graduate seminar (and indeed the graduate program) as a venue for a Darwinian process of natural selection and survival of the fittest, wherein the students are encouraged to be "red in tooth and claw."

Of course, graduate seminars must encourage careful thinking and skillful analysis. Graduate programs do involve processes whereby some students succeed and others fail. Students who are ill-suited or inappropriately skilled for an academic career should not be encouraged to continue on, especially if they are incurring large amounts of debt. However, that process of selection is the responsibility of the graduate faculty, who are grading seminar projects and judging students' qualifying and special field examinations. It is not useful or responsible to encourage students to attack, demean, or "toughen up" each other. While vigorous debate should always be welcomed, encouraging hypercompetitiveness and combativeness among graduate students simply creates and re-creates an academic culture of egotism, suspicion, and generally antisocial behavior. We reap the harvest of that training in our own overly contentious faculty meetings and vicious departmental squabbles.

Even in graduate classes and seminars, communal thinking must be encouraged and rewarded. While it sounds very "undergraduate," I regularly build group work into meetings of even my doctoral-level classes. To have students work in pairs or trios to generate an interpretation of a text or analytical response to an issue or question is to train them in the skills that I want to see in new colleagues: those of negotiation, compromise, a willingness to agree to disagree, and an ability to present to a larger group the main points of and most compelling reasoning behind a group opinion. I do not demand consensus and certainly allow for expressions of dissent in a group report back to the class. However, what I do expect is a willingness to engage in dialogue and to articulate some shared goals or points of agreement, even if significant differences remain. As students respond to each other's work in class—whether in group settings or in individual presentations—I also ask that they commend what is positive and successful even if they express disagreement or find problems with an argument or a specific line of reasoning. Productive conversation always demands a dynamic of generosity even in the midst of significant disagreement.

Similarly, I never disallow collaborative work even in final seminar or class projects. I allow students to choose the format that best suits their talents and personalities. Frankly, I have never enjoyed collaborative writing or research. I love working with colleagues in meetings and on various institutional tasks, but then I also relish the time I spend alone writing and following an idiosyncratic train of thought. However, to those students who do find in collaborative writing and project design a form of work that they can love, I say, "Go for it." I remind them, of course, that most academic careers in the humanities have not succeeded or failed to date on the basis of collaborative research and writing (I can think of only a handful in my field of English—Sandra Gilbert and Susan Gubar, being preeminent). However, that situation may change in the future, and there is no reason why students should not experiment with collaborative work to see if it suits their styles, especially as it may lead to collaborative teaching efforts (which many of them express a great interest in). Of course, they must also acquire the self-confidence and skills necessary to pursue capstone projects (theses or dissertations) that will usually be solely authored, but the ability to collaborate is such a rare and laudable skill in the academy that I would never disallow students the opportunity to exercise it. Indeed, no matter how much we encourage collaboration, I have full confidence that the ability to work alone and in self-interested fashion will never be endangered in our profession.

In Research and Dissertation Projects

Even if our students' capstone projects and much of their other research that leads to publication or presentation is very often solely conducted and single-authored (especially in the humanities and social sciences), we can still impress upon them how such work is always done in dialogic fashion. In every field of research, one's own articulation must engage with previous articulations. I stress to students always that they are, through their work, entering a conversation with their predecessors and their peers. They must understand and acknowledge previous contributions to the conversation, its norms and points of disagreement, and then they must prove themselves to be responsible and credible contributors to the ongoing dialogue. Conceptualizing their contributions in this way means that they can avoid the trap of thinking that they must provide the "last word" or definitive statement on a topic or research question. I remind them often that the conversation that they are entering will continue long after they have contributed to it, hopefully with a generous acknowledgment of their contribution, but in ways over which they have no control. As I stress in *The Academic Self,* it is never useful to obsess over the response or acclaim that we hope to receive for a given project or piece of writing. For graduate students, too, it is best to focus on the responsible and skillful completion of the project itself, and the joys that can be derived from pursuing it. Its impact or reception will always be chancy. In fact, framing all of their work in that way helps reduce the likelihood of the always dreaded "writer's block," which so often is the result of a quest for an impossible perfection.

Of course, many students do want to publish and disseminate their contributions to a wider audience, to participate in conversations beyond those of their classes or home departments. Certainly, as they contemplate going on the job market or building a career after they secure a job, publication is key to establishing their credibility as recognized contributors to the knowledge base in their fields. It is helpful, even then, to emphasize that such dissemination is part of a conversational, even collegial, process. They are always writing or speaking to an audience whose needs must be understood and met. Furthermore, they are engaged in dialogic exchanges with conference organizers, editors, and publishers, the success of which can lead to opportunities to disseminate or that can lead to rejection. In this way, all successful research and writing has to involve a decentering of the author from the position of sole authority. She or he must listen carefully as well as express skillfully. I stress to students that if they do not learn first how to listen carefully to feedback from faculty and from their peers, then they are certainly doomed when they have to work with readers' reports; outside evaluations on grant proposals; and other responses inherent to the research, dissemination, and publication process. In every graduate class I teach, I remind them of this conversational dynamic as they work on their final projects. It infuses all aspects of a successful research life—from the conceptualization of a project through writing to an imagined or known group of readers to the mechanics of working with funding agencies, editors, and a publishing production team.

In the Professionalization of Graduate Students

This emphasis on conversational skills and commitments allows us then to fine-tune also our definition of what "professionalization" actually means. Certainly in the venues above—the classroom and in research mentorship—we work to make our students more aware of the norms and best practices of academic professional life. But the graduate programs that are most concerned with meeting their students' needs attend also to that professionalization process by offering seminars, roundtables, workshops, and other activities to students intent on or just thinking about pursuing an academic career. In all of these it is important to note that aspiring academics are not only entering the conversation represented by their research fields, but also the conversation of a dynamic and multifaceted profession.

This means encouraging literal conversations among graduate students and recent graduates who have taken a wide variety of positions—from high-profile academic, to teaching-centered, to those in the publishing industry and a wide variety of nonacademic fields. I started this chapter by noting that I had never heard from or about individuals who had taken jobs like the one I eventually took. Certainly I could have sought out those individuals on my own (though I didn't know them personally, since they were not part of my cohort group), but it is also true that those individuals were not generally recognized as ones to emulate.

One hopes, given the terrible prospects that most new PhDs face today as they enter the academic job market, that such snobbishness has waned. As a caveat, however, I would never go so far as to say that we should tell students that "any job" is better than "no job" or that they should simply "take what they can get." Conversations with individuals in a variety of postgraduate school positions can lead to much better-informed choices by job candidates. Some individuals would be terribly mismatched with certain positions—weak teachers who live for research should not take positions at teaching universities unless they are willing to reprioritize and devote their energies to improving their pedagogies. Similarly, I have known superb teachers with modest research skills who have taken wholly inappropriate positions at prestigious universities and then lost those jobs for low research productivity during third-year or tenure reviews (unfortunately, they sometimes got their jobs in the first place because they were able to—and were counseled to—market themselves within certain highly sought-after identity political fields but with no recognition of their own individual needs or abilities). A discussion of who will be happy and will succeed where *must* be part of any broad conversation on the academic profession.

Furthermore, it is important for students to understand and discuss the ways departments and college function, their substrata of committees, rules, and processes. When students fill out evaluation forms in my classes, many have never even been told that those are reviewed by an elected faculty committee charged with making recommendations on tenure, promotion, and pay raises. Similarly, when students offer suggestions about changes to individual classes or the design of a program, they usually are unaware of how such changes are instituted through curricular and other oversight bodies. There are ample opportunities for us to discuss institutional governance and service possibilities if we see those as worthy of discussion. They are a significant component of the "text" of an academic career that we must help students read and understand.

Indeed, it is vital to invite students into conversation on such matters as often and as early as possible. At the beginning of every meeting of every graduate class I teach, I ask if there are any questions on the minds of the students regarding their program, general professional issues or processes, or the often unexplained norms of academic life. Even if students are sometimes too shy to ask what they really want to know in class, their recognition of my willingness to address such issues means they often show up during office hours to ask what they consider an embarrassing question ("how do hiring committees make decisions?" or "what do you say in a cover letter when you send out an article for consideration?"). We have to let students know that we are willing to share information with them in an honest and practical manner. As I have insisted repeatedly here, we must be open texts for them to read and learn from in their own processes of professional interpretation and skill-building.

And I believe it would be useful to build some of the expectations above into the desired outcomes of our graduate programs. In fact, I haven't heard of any programs that articulate specific goals for professionalization processes, but I think we should be asking what specifically we wish the end product to be of those seminars, workshops, and other conversations about academic life. I would offer that an overarching goal might be to *help our students become more supple and skilled participants in the wide variety of conversations that comprise an academic career.* By necessity, acquiring this conversational skill means learning the value of being both multivoiced and open to the perspectives of others.

This bears some explanation. By multivoiced I am not implying that students should learn to be Machiavellian or duplicitous. Rather, I mean that all of us who are thriving in our careers have learned to speak within a wide variety of contexts and to choose our language carefully depending upon the venue. I would never speak in class as I do in some of my more theoretically dense writings. I would never speak to administrators from other departments as I do to those in my home department who use the same terms and points of reference that I do. Finally, I would never speak to the public exactly as I would to a scholarly audience at a conference. Being multivoiced in this way means being aware of our conversation partners' needs and placing their need to understand above our own desire to express ourselves in intellectually self-serving ways.

And this is, in fact, an important component of being open to the perspectives of others. Yet that openness also means allowing one's own beliefs, values, and opinions to be challenged and transformed by contact with those of conversation partners, which is Kögler's point in the quotations above. This does not mean being unwilling to defend one's beliefs (whether on matters concerning the ethical treatment of others or on minute points of interpretation), but it does mean being able to position oneself at least partially outside of oneself in the process of conversational exchange. It means, for example, working to understand how the general public perceives the academy (and the issue of tenure, for example). It means trying to see the world through the eyes of a different generation of professors who may use very different methodologies or theoretical touchstones in their work. It means listening to other committee members from different departments and trying to understand the assumptions that they bring to a shared task. Above all, it means seeing one's own sacredly held positions as ones that exist in a landscape of positions, many of which are also sacredly held. For those beliefs that we *do* return to with renewed commitment after that process of conversational exchange, we are often even better able to explain and defend them in subsequent conversations. This is true in our interactions with the public; with colleagues in department meetings; and with administrators over matters of budget, personnel reviews, or programmatic design.

As I've suggested in earlier chapters and as *The Power of Dialogue* argues cogently, this is a hermeneutic move, and indeed, one indicator of "success" in our graduate programs is the extent to which our students understand their professional lives as a series of such hermeneutic moves. Through the professional conversations that they enter, they are able to reflect upon their standpoint epistemologies and adjust their performances in a variety of roles and venues. As teachers in training, they enter conversations with peers and with students that afford opportunities to hone their pedagogies. As researchers in training, they receive feedback from classmates, faculty, audience members at conferences, and reviewers at journals and presses that provide external perspectives on their work.

Indeed, only by listening carefully to and changing (sometimes significantly and sometimes incrementally) by way of those external points of reference are researchers able to fine-tune even their most revolutionary and iconoclastic ideas (no doubt, even Nietzsche, from chapter 1's discussion, could have benefited from that process). Furthermore, as future committee members and participants in faculty governance bodies, they must learn to speak with a wide variety of colleagues whose different opinions and disciplinary perspectives will challenge and should enlarge their own. Finally, this dynamic is especially important when dealing with the larger public in ways that I will explore in chapter 5. As Kögler notes, it is this hermeneutic practice that "constitutes the move away from the socially situated self toward the reflexively critical self. Because this shift turns unrecognized distinctions into ones that are understood, it can be the starting point for directed and reflective social action" (275).

And to make my own "meta" move now, this is not only true for graduate student success, it is also true for programmatic success. Solipsism and isolationism can plague graduate programs as well as individuals within programs. Faculty who fall out of conversation with their fields of specialization, their colleagues, and their students will be increasingly anachronistic and ineffective. Programs and departments that fail to engage dialogically and continuously with the needs of their students, faculty, and college- and university-level administrators will also become ineffective and certainly will be institutionally disadvantaged. But as important as these local conversations are, equally crucial is an engagement with the conversation represented by the exchange of ideas and identity-based information provided by other programs across the country. This, I believe, is one of the most important hermeneutic moves a graduate program (and really, any department or institution) can make, to see itself as part of a landscape of programs, and by way of that "meta" move, arrive at a sense of honed mission.

This happens most commonly today when outside evaluators or visitors are brought in to assess a program's design and operations, and make recommendations for its improvement. While outside evaluations can easily go awry and should never be taken as hard-and-fast "truth" (simply as useful information that augments other information available), I believe they are essential to a program and department's vitality. When I serve as outside evaluator, I always attempt to commend what is unique about a program, what makes it (or potentially makes it) an important component of a national, regional, or local array (one might even say "menu") of programs that would appeal to students in compelling ways. My comments are presented as limited suggestions only, but, I always hope, add to what would otherwise be a local and more limited conversation. Educational microsystems always languish and deteriorate if they remain artificially closed. Isolationism can be functional in temporary ways, but in the long term, it proves to be disastrous. In fact, I have sometimes been brought in, far too late, to evaluate programs that had become practically nonfunctional because they had, for decades even, internally reinforced their own limited perceptions and behavior patterns.

Indeed, outside reviews often take place only every five years or so and therefore hardly provide a consistent-enough stream of data for programs to rely upon them for self-assessment and improvement. That data should be sought out also by administrators who regularly attend professional studies conferences, visit other programs and campuses to exchange information, and allow their own assumptions and practices to be brought into question through those exchanges. Every dean and department chair undergoes (or should undergo) periodic evaluation by those to whom she or he reports. Part of that evaluation should attend closely to the ways in which the administrator under review maintains the currency of her or his knowledge about similar institutional units across the nation, and how often she or he engages in conversations with administrators from peer institutions. When we are evaluated as scholars (through the publication review process or evaluation by tenure and promotion committees), we are assessed on the currency and depth of our knowledge. The same should be true of administrators of graduate programs, who must demonstrate that they continuously refresh their knowledge base through research into the fields represented by their administrative appointments and through information sharing with colleagues holding similar positions.

I have long believed that this inside/outside move—from local norms, desires, and beliefs, to a broad engagement with other programs' strengths and weaknesses—should lead to a sharpened (and continuously revisited) sense of focus and identity for any institution and unit within an institution. Even if a department or program is extraordinarily well funded, it cannot be all things to all people. As I indicate above, graduate programs, like universities and departments, must make difficult choices about how to allocate resources and how to "position" themselves in the landscape of programs locally, regionally, and nationally. A lack of purpose and priority usually means a squandering of money and talent. Setting up little institutes that complement nothing else in the department, bringing in speakers who will attract no audience, running little conferences that have nothing to do with anything else the program is engaged in—these are common ways that energy and resources are expended with little payoff. Focusing and clarifying a sense of identity are keys to any unit's success, and that identity can only be shaped in conversation with the expressed identities of other units with which it coexists and often competes.

This process of focusing and (to use an inevitable marketing term) packaging will often run contrary to some faculty's sense of an ideal program or one that reflects their own interests and specializations. Yet every process of strategic planning demands a willingness on some individuals' parts to sacrifice their own self-interest for the broader interests of the program, and this may present one of the most difficult tests of collegiality that a group will face. If an English program looks at its current strengths and offerings, and determines that its clearest identity base is in American literature, I, as a Victorian literature specialist, may have to accept that fact and give up my claim to be represented as a key component of the department's focus areas and commitments. Of course all programs should train students in ways that are both broadly based and deep in certain areas, which means I will always have an important role to play in undergraduate and graduate education in my department. However, I may be peripheral, finally, to the department's main sense of mission and distinction.

Certainly in the case of small programs with limited resources, a process of focusing is key to survival and to the placement of its graduates. I am very positively impressed, for example, with the decision made by the English Department of Illinois State University (which is not the flagship institution in that state) to focus much of its PhD program's energies on children's literature and culture. Having sat on numerous hiring committees looking for highly qualified candidates in that field (as we were adding depth to the teacher training program at CSU Northridge), I knew how dire the need was for a program devoted to filling that niche, one that many programs dismissed as lightweight or beneath their notice. Illinois State is now producing PhDs who are highly sought after nationally, who are writing important books in the field, and who are exceptionally well trained to teach at the regional comprehensive universities that educate many of this nation's K-12 teachers. ISU's practicality and willingness to focus itself to meet a clear national need demonstrates how a relatively small and modestly funded department can decide to add uniquely to the panoply of American graduate programs, one in which there is far too much duplication and which turns out graduates who often run into terrible problems on the job market.

Not all programs will define themselves that narrowly. But it makes no sense to try to do everything equally well. That vagueness does not allow one to make smart choices in distinguishing among relatively similar job candidates: does a given candidate add clearly to the department's strengths or does that candidate do work that is highly specialized in ways that neither broaden nor deepen the department's course offerings? I am not advocating a uniformity of perspective in a department; there are usually many ways a department can work toward a sense of complementarity among their faculty and activities without reaching a drab and intellectually static sameness. If anything, individuals approaching similar research questions but from significantly different methodological and historical perspectives would be an ideal scenario for productive collegial conversation and graduate student training.

Furthermore, a vagueness of purpose and identity works against the interests of prospective students who need to be able to choose wisely from among the many graduate program possibilities nationally and with some assurance that they will find complementary course offerings that will allow them to develop a well-supported field of specialization. A clear sense of focus or programmatic priority means that when students arrive at the department, they will find speakers, colloquia, conferences, and events that further support their work in a given field. This same sense of focus also means that admissions committees will have the ability to choose from among applicants the ones whose projected interests and projects can be supported reasonably with course offerings and other activities. It is unwise and unfair for a department to admit a student, no matter how well qualified, who desperately wants to specialize in Victorian literature, if the department knows that it will only rarely be able to offer a course in that area.

These are difficult decisions that every graduate program should make. It is clearly a process wherein a faculty's ability to engage in careful yet productive conversation may be tested in clear and dramatic ways. That some groups of faculty would fail such a test again demonstrates how a dialogically based hermeneutic process *should be* part of every future faculty member's training. Indeed, as a department engages in the discussions mentioned above, it should invite into the dialogue advanced graduate students. This inclusion adds important student-based perspectives on the topic of program design and also provides yet another venue for professionalization.

Providing that opportunity for students to participate in programmatic decision making and planning offers them a window into yet another area of professional activity with which they might otherwise have no experience: administration. We rarely talk with students about career paths that would include administrative appointments. Part of that silence may be due to our own suspicion of administrators as likely evildoers and part of it may be our prejudicial belief that administrators are simply failed scholars. Why would we talk to students about the possibility that one day they might be a department chair or associate dean if that assumes their inability to make a name for themselves as researchers?

However, if we demonstrate to students that administration is itself an intellectual activity, that successful administration demands the same hermeneutic moves required by successful scholarship and teaching, we do them and ourselves a service in preparing the future leaders of our programs and institutions. To allow them to participate in processes through which local needs and priorities are placed in dialogue with broader professional norms and trends, in which the profession itself is viewed as textually rich and interesting, and through which an energetic conversation emerges that involves a testing of evidence bases and a honing of interpretive assertions, is to ensure that we will have future colleagues, department chairs, and deans with whom we can interact productively.

We in the academy work in one of the very few professions where we have near complete control over the training of our own future colleagues. Law firms hire from law schools; engineering firms from engineering programs; high schools hire from university programs in education. However, we in higher education hire almost exclusively from among those whom we collectively train. That gives us more control over the skills and attitudes of our future colleagues than practically any other field and more *responsibility* for changing what we do not like or what we perceive as failings. If we want our programs to produce a different type of professional, we do not have to convince any external body or group to take action—we only have to convince ourselves and our university colleagues that change is desirable.

The question then remains, what type of colleague do you want, and how is any program with which you have influence meeting the needs of its students and our collective future through their professionalization? We should all think of ourselves as agents of change in this arena. However, if we are tenured, especially, we have the responsibility to raise such difficult topics and initiate conversation on issues that may threaten some faculty. That risk taking, in research, teaching, and here, service, is the only justification for the job security that tenure represents and is even part of the contours of a career in the academy as we should discuss it with our graduate students. The period leading up to tenure is when one demonstrates one's skills at teaching, service, and research activities, the period after tenure is when one can most safely assume leadership in dealing with difficult issues and emerging crises. Sometimes we simply cannot wait that long before becoming agents of change, but certainly after tenure, we have no excuse for letting problems fester.

While the stereotype of the shy and fumbling professor has elicited laughs on television and in films for many years, in reality, ours is a more social and performance-based career than just about any other, outside of politics, public relations, and trial law. While gregariousness is hardly a job requisite, responsible and effective communication skills are. Our thoughtful participation in a variety of overlapping and discrete conversations will determine our collective fate as a profession and the health and stability of our individual departments and institutions. We must face that fact and train our newest colleagues in the skills necessary to meet all of those challenges.

chapter four

Building a Vibrant Department and University Community

*W*HILE THE two preceding chapters examined the crucial work we do as teachers and mentors of students, I want to turn now to that equally vital component of our professional lives: research and intellectual exchange in a community of scholars. Indeed, we cannot be effective teachers if we are isolated from the dynamism of our intellectual fields. Even if we do not choose to make the publication of research a top priority in our professional lives (and so long as we understand the career implications of such a choice), it is still irresponsible for any of us to allow our knowledge bases to become outdated and our perspectives on/in our fields of specialization anachronistic. In contexts where research is institutionally de-emphasized, as is the case at some teaching-intensive colleges and universities, an anachronistic knowledge base among faculty still should never be institutionally validated. In fact, when the responsible instruction of students is held as the highest priority, it is especially important that such instruction be delivered with intellectual currency and vitality.

In this chapter I am not urging a heightened commitment to a "publish or perish" mandate. Publication requirements should always reflect institutional contexts (especially teaching loads) and scholarship may take many different formats depending upon those contexts and individual talents and preferences. I have spent the past two years participating in a wide-ranging discussion on this topic as a member of the Modern Language Association's Task Force on Evaluating Scholarship for Tenure and Promotion. Our Task Force report, available online at www. mla.org, recommends strongly that colleges and universities recognize the great diversity of formats that scholarship can take (including electronic, pedagogically useful, and collaborative) and that all institutions allow multiple pathways for young academics to meet scholarship requirements for tenure and promotion, ones that should be institutionally appropriate, flexible, and transparent.

Yet my point here is much broader than the ones just mentioned, because I am looking beyond the career needs of the individual academic. As communities of teachers/scholars/institutional citizens, publication is only one way that we participate in intellectual exchange. Indeed, that same participation can also be achieved through reading widely and discussing what we read, through conference attendance and the delivery there of scholarly papers, and through programs that bring in speakers and writers who are doing exciting new work and who share that work with faculty and students. In the coming pages, I will discuss a wide variety of ways that individual faculty and administrators can be of great importance to the vitality of an institution, but not only for the prominence of their individual research achievements. In developing the themes of previous chapters, I will emphasize instead how the individual academic community member should also invest in the work of fostering a lively and productive intellectual environment for her or his colleagues and students. There is no professional venue across the landscape of the academy—from community colleges through elite research universities—where such an atmosphere is not central to achieving the mission of the institution.

As always, the success of this process of building intellectual dynamism and support among colleagues depends upon our commitment to the central value of "academic community" and our willingness to reflect on what that concept means, how it is nurtured, and also how it can be threatened or undermined. To my mind, this is the most important aspect of the work being done today in the field of "professional studies": the fostering of a dialogue concerning why we do what we do as academics, how we variously find and make meaning in our professional lives and careers, and how we can exercise agency in choosing to do things differently in our departments and broader institutional settings. And these choices and the discussions that surround them must begin at the level of the individual faculty member or administrator, even if their success also always depends upon effective group planning and coalition building.

If we are unhappy with the atmosphere in our departments, if we find that our communities suffer from intellectual or pedagogical inertia and other dysfunctions, then, as members of that community, we are partially responsible for that atmosphere and must take some measure of responsibility for changing it. As I have argued elsewhere, we too often excuse our own complicities with the status quo with an over-quick allusion to hegemonic power structures, constricting institutional norms or mandates, and debilitating inequities in our positions vis-à-vis our universities, colleges, administrators, and senior colleagues. However, unless we sort out the extent to which we as individuals also participate in perpetuating any deadening or dysfunctional forces and relationships, we will simply remain victims and, to some degree, self-victimizers. *We always bear responsibility* for the communities of which we are a part. Perhaps they are oppressive or dysfunctional, and on rare occasions, even irredeemably so. But we cannot know that without first assuming that we can contribute positively to their metamorphosis and their significant improvement, even if that improvement is incrementally realized.

I hesitate to invoke Dr. Phil McGraw here because his summary judgments and bullying style can be so disturbing, and especially troubling is his daily talk-show invocation of traditional and oppressive notions of gender. However, that being said, there is still considerable use value in his repeated emphasis on "responsibility taking." And no doubt part of the reason for his stunning growth in popularity in recent years (since I first mentioned him in *The Academic Self*) is that what he says meets a certain need at this moment for a general reminder that we often have the ability to change our lives and our communities through modestly defined goal setting, in spite of inherited situations and social circumstance. Individually, we have to start with an assumption of our own agency, however cautiously and tentatively we may wish to proceed in attempting to exercise it. Otherwise, we will have to be content with the status quo as others have defined it.

Thus the overarching emphasis of this chapter and the next is going to be assuming responsibility for change in our communities—in our roles, among others, as colleagues, administrators, and publicly engaged intellectuals. And what we bear responsibility for fostering is what I consider the cornerstone of a vibrant and productive academic community: dialogue. But why, you might ask, would I even link "productivity" to "vibrancy" in community-building and nurturance? By productivity I do not mean efficiency or some quasi-Fordist emphasis on quantitative output (indeed, that is a stressor that I will discuss later). But I do believe that a vibrant university community is one that does produce new types of knowledge, new forms of critical awareness in students, and new or usefully different answers to compelling questions. Vibrancy, rooted in the Latin *vibrare*, carries with it by definition movement, quickness, and the humming quality of activity and creation. Such vibrancy is always rooted in our communication with others: with the authors whom we are reading; with the work of previous researchers; and even more important, with students, off- and on-campus colleagues, administrators, and the public at large.

In fact, all existence is inherently dialogic, even that of the seemingly isolated researcher. Phenomenologically speaking, we are in constant dialogue with all that surrounds us, as we process incoming information, adjust to the microlevel—even mundane—demands we encounter in our academic and personal lives, and provide the information and make the demands that help comprise the daily lives of others. This is a dialogue that we can embrace and invest in or nervously deny and lose some degree of agency as we enact and participate in it. Thus responsibility taking is key here, for again, the ways that we either collude with or challenge the behaviors and assumptions that can demoralize and disable us are, to a degree always worth reflecting on, within our own control.

This returns us to Gadamer's notion of dialogue and critical agency, and specifically, dialogue's usefulness in a process of community-building within an academic institution. In his 1977 autobiography *Philosophical Apprenticeships*, Gadamer speaks in detail about his academic work life, as a professor, as an administrator (he was a department chair, dean, and university rector/president), and as a colleague. He discusses, for example, the particular necessity of working to create community across academic departments, stating, "Today, in the face of the fragmentation of the giant universities, such interdisciplinary efforts have a new significance" (122). He writes of his work at the University of Marburg in the 1930s in organizing and participating in "one-hour lecture[s] on something of interest from one's own discipline" "for listeners from all faculties" (122). While serving as professor and later dean at the University of Heidelberg, he created what he called a "home circle," in which a dozen or so people would gather to discuss texts of common interest, adding that "[t]here was no 'teacher' among us; it was always a free exchange, and we all learned a good deal from it" (140). He comments that "[a]nother feature that I introduced into . . . Heidelberg . . . was that of regular guest lecturers . . . because I wanted to give the philosophy students an opportunity to get to know other teachers, and the discussions that followed were good tests for both participants and listeners" (140). He did all of this while serving as an administrator and also teaching and trying to pursue his own research. As he says, "This is in any case not easy for an academic teacher, and even in those times it demanded a consistent budgeting of personal time, although the number of students and the whole style of the university were not yet comparable with those of today's mass universities" (139).

Obviously, we today, especially those of us teaching in mass universities, need even more active attention to that process of community-building. In Gadamer's commentary we already see an attention to the practical aspects of nurturing and maintaining community. One critic remarks: "Despite having lived through a century that witnessed and participated in two world wars, and having experienced the upheavals of the new social movements of the interwar and post–World War II years, Gadamer lived a markedly insular, scholarly life" (Code, *Feminist Interpretations of Hans-Georg Gadamer,* 3), but I beg to differ. If we denigrate as "insular" the work that can be done within institutions and as colleagues and administrators, then only those of us who take to the streets or perhaps march into battle are valued as agents of "real" change. In my opinion, that is far too narrow a purview for our work and for our possible attachment to processes of social transformation. In fact, it may keep us from attending to the local, departmental, or home institutional needs by setting up a false binary of "big" and important versus "small" and insignificant. That can be an excuse and yet another (witting or unwitting) means of responsibility avoidance. And though I have been tarrying here at the level of the macro and theoretical, our work at the microlevels of our departments, colleges, and universities matters tremendously. We cannot all lead mass uprisings against fascist regimes or institutionalized oppression, but we can all find our own ways of improving our own professional contexts and those of our colleagues and students. Indeed, we all share that as a core professional duty.

I title this chapter "Building a Vibrant Department and University Community," but is there not inscribed within that phrasing an inherent tension between "vibrancy" (that which is alive and open to possibilities) and "community" (that which is exclusionary and homogenizing)? Indeed, they are only compatible if we think of community as an always artificial construct whose boundaries must be porous and welcoming, whose goal is not consensus (and which is not the point of Gadamer's conversational model, either), but rather an always dynamic state, which the critic J. Hillis Miller (echoing Bill Readings) has called for in his model of a professional community of dissensus,

> in which there is great diversity, and in which professors and students have goals with particular and very different positions, vocations, and commitments or ways of doing things, ones that they, I would hope, do with their whole heart. All of these individuals could reside amicably within the same [institution], if each is courteous and respectful of those people who hold positions with which he or she disagrees. This does not mean that forceful argument should not occur, but that this disagreement need not have consensus as its horizon. ("Vital Diversity," 229)

Community does not depend upon consensus—a fact that bears repeating—*community is not consensus*. Community is a conversational process, a "becoming" that is never fully achieved, a process that we must choose and continuously commit to. And if that sounds tautological, then so be it. Some of my readers will have deeply held spiritual or other beliefs that may provide foundational support for the cause of community-building and neighborly love. But for those of us who are skeptical of transcendental truths, what we nevertheless have are tautologies to which we can decide to ascribe importance and meaning, and for which we bear responsibility in choosing and defending for their life-, justice-, and community-affirming qualities. In my worldview, at least, existence always precedes essence, and it also always precedes the ethical choices that I am nevertheless called upon to make.

Community is conversation, I have said, and the devil in the details, so to speak, is how to create structures and venues that allow for conversation to occur. Much of our work may be done alone in preparing classes, grading papers, conducting our research, and writing our articles or books. Some of us team teach and some of us coauthor works with colleagues, but many of us spend a lot of time in silent, solitary forms of professional activity. I will leave it to another time and to others who feel more forcefully about those norms to challenge the solitary nature of our teaching and much of our writing. My reminder here is that even as we, or if we, disrupt those norms, we also always need structures that bring us together in larger venues of conversation and community-building. Coauthoring and team teaching does not a community make. Indeed, if confined solely to two or a few faculty, it can contribute to divisiveness and a lack of broadly cast dialogue.

Especially in what Gadamer calls our "fragmented, giant universities," it is imperative that we create diverse nexuses of shared interest and conversational energy. Some of what I suggest in the coming pages may appear rather commonplace and obvious, but I have little faith that simply because something is obvious means necessarily that it is being done regularly. I encounter often, in my commentary on the profession, a "oh, yes, yes, yes, that . . . of course" response that usually means that whatever I have suggested is not going to be done because either it was tried once in the distant past and met with little success then or because it is considered so very elementary that presumably we have progressed far beyond such a primitive state and rudimentary set of needs. We very smart academics are also very good at thinking our way out of, and talking our way out of, responsibility. And that dismissive "oh yes, yes, yes" response is one signal that we may be doing so.

We can choose otherwise. Even if we do not agree necessarily on our approaches to our research, our fiscal priorities for our departments or colleges, or proposed curricular changes, we nevertheless can choose to come together in instances of common inquiry and shared discovery that can help provide ballast when our chosen and sometimes highly fragile community is threatened by internal or external stressors. And, indeed, those choices to commit to community often represent thoughtful responses to actual conversational openers. In other words, a department chair, a dean, or a motivated colleague must often ask her or his colleagues for communally focused energy and renewed intellectual, collegial commit-ment. Those interlocutors must then decide how they will respond. But wherever it leads, the process always starts with a decision to try to elicit subtly or perhaps even to request explicitly such a commitment, and that initial decision represents academic leadership at its most crucial and, unfortunately, most rare. Missed or dismissed opportunities for academic community-building by well-positioned administrators in particular are all too common, even though intellectually and professionally irresponsible.

The call may have to come, then, from a newly tenured associate professor, a new senior colleague, or even a working group of junior col-leagues. However, the decision-making process does not end with the choice to issue and respond to such a call. To build and maintain a com-munity means also choosing an open and inquisitive attitude toward one's colleagues. That attitude is our responsibility also. Gadamer's model of dialogue "requires that one does not try to argue the other person down but that one really considers the weight of the other's opinion. . . . [It] consists not in trying to discover the weakness of what is said, but in bringing out its real strength. It is not the art of arguing . . . but the art of thinking" (*Truth and Method*, 367). As we embrace that openness, there is yet another aspect to attitudinal responsibility that even Gadamer misses in his otherwise astute commentary. Feminist philosopher Veronica Vasterling supplements his model with a useful reminder that partners in dialogue often speak out of diverse social power positions, backgrounds, and perspectives, and that productive dialogue must also always include "critical reflection on the situatedness of understanding" ("Postmodern Hermeneutics?" 178); she reminds us that we should listen to others and attempt to understand not only their opinion but also "where they are coming from," so to speak. I will have more to say later about those dif-ferent "situations" we are in, as sometimes tenured and sometimes junior (therefore vulnerable) academics.

Yet again, and not denying the devils in those details, the necessity is not only for a productive attitude toward but also the dynamic occa-sion for dialogue. Vague calls will produce no results. Concrete plans and actual conversational occasions are crucial. These can take several use-ful forms and formats, ones that I will discuss now with reference to my work as a department chair at California State University, Northridge; as cofounder of a lesbian, gay, bisexual, and transgender studies institute there; as director of a Humanities Interdisciplinary Studies program there; and as a faculty member and now administrator at West Virginia University.

In all of those roles and in the sixteen years I have spent employed in the academy, I have found that generally we do not often enough read, listen to, and appreciate the research and pedagogical work of our colleagues, especially in our home departments. Often, we don't even know what our colleague across the hall is working on. One of the simplest ways that any one of us can help build a vibrant community is by creating venues and events to share with each other that work, which is often done in solitary fashion. And these can take several formats, each of which can operate as one strand in a web of institutional community.

One of the easiest and most fundamental structures that we can create to serve as a basis for community is a regular occasion in which we formally present and respond to each other's scholarship (which I think of as including pedagogical innovations as well as more traditional research). This is inexpensive and often can be created by simply sending an e-mail request to colleagues on a list serve. All that is required is a place, a time, and a small group willing to devote an hour a month to making it happen. However, the rewards for such a small investment can be extraordinary. At Northridge, I instituted monthly brown-bag lunches in which one or two people would share, by reading aloud, a relatively brief excerpt from a finished work or work-in-progress, followed by an energetic question-and-answer session. Since, in those instances, we were coming together because of a shared interest in lesbian and gay studies, but also coming from many different departments and disciplines (English, philosophy, library science, anthropology), they usually provided occasions for us to talk about the methodological norms and discover the presuppositional differences of our very diverse fields. This allowed for a synergy of sharing new information and also of learning about different methodologies (disrupting thereby the sanctity or "reality" of our own). It created a conversation across disciplines that also expanded the scope of conversation within the disciplines.

In advocating the creation of such occasions, I am not arguing for interdisciplinarity as a singular goal or mandated way of being in our institutions. Our departments and disciplinary structures are vital to the creation of new knowledge; research often demands specialized language and both references and builds upon common assumptions and method-ologies. However, only the most arrogant of practitioners in a given disci-pline would claim to have sole access to the truth of social, cultural, and lived physical existence. To create interdisciplinary conversations around topics that necessarily reference many different avenues of inquiry—race, gender, sexualities, power, intellectualism, justice, ethics, etc.—is to add immeasurably to the otherwise discrete, limited perspectives that we bring to the topic. It is not to deny the legitimacy of the worth that one indi-vidual, coming out of psychology or history, may bring to a conversation. It is simply to remind all participants that their individual perspectives are methodologically circumscribed. Such exchanges *out of diversity* can lead to conversation at its most dynamic and exciting.

Bringing people together in this way, sometimes from campus units that otherwise are unknown to us, also helps demonstrate to us just how hard others were working (and what they are working on) across our institutions. Other than occasionally interacting with anthropologists on a faculty committee, I often have no knowledge of the work being done in that department housed in another campus building. Ignorance under-mines community. Indeed, far too often I have encountered the destruc-tive force of individuals within institutions thinking that they alone are overtaxed or stressed, that somehow others have loads of squandered or inefficiently used time. This even plagues entire departments, where the commonplace might be that "we here in Political Science are working like maniacs, but those guys in the Sociology Department aren't doing much of anything." To hear what your colleague is working on in her or his research is to begin to fill in those blank spaces in the other's life about which we know nothing: those hours that you spend sitting in front of a computer screen or at your desk and that I may misunderstand as somehow easier or less productive than my hours spent similarly. To learn more about each other's work, to hear it, mull it over, offer our responses, and learn something new through it, is finally to renew ties of respect that can too often be threatened by the internal and external stressors that are common in academic life.

And this is even more readily accomplished through a different varia-tion on the format I just mentioned, one in which we more proactively workshop our projects and research even when they are in very rough form. At both Northridge and at West Virginia University I've created

Faculty Research Groups within the English departments in which individuals bring to the group a piece of writing on which they would like advice or constructive response, circulated to all group members a week before we meet to discuss it. This is healthy and helpful not only for the individual whose writing is being work-shopped, who often receives very useful commentary, but also by helping shift the focus and dynamic of faculty interactions. By sharing a rough draft, I admit to you my human fallibility, my humility, my need for your help. By responding sensitively and generously to that rough work, you demonstrate to me your concern and respect, your acknowledgment of the importance of what I am doing (that it is worth your time and effort to contribute to it), and (depending on how sensitively and self-reflectively you offer your advice) your recognition of the expertise that I bring to my work that you can contribute to but not claim mastery over.

That is, in microcosmic form, what a "vibrant department and university community" consists of: connections of respect, generosity, and always renewed understanding. We do not have to agree with each other on department policy or pursue projects that are even remotely similar. However, we do have to know something about each other's lives and perspectives, and come to some acknowledgment of the significance of each other's work, even if it is radically dissimilar. This is how "dissensus" can function on a day-to-day basis. Thus, I have received superb advice on my work in Victorian studies from scholars in American and medieval literature. Even if the individual responding knows little about George Eliot, she or he often gives excellent advice on the clarity of my argument and the methods I use in my analysis. We can be each other's best readers and editors.

This may be one of those instances where this book's readers say "oh, yes, yes, yes. . . ." But how often do we enact this, do we live this practice of sharing our work and our generous responses with each other, especially in a small- or medium-sized group context? When a dozen people, more or less, come together monthly, to read each other's work, talk about it, and offer their responses, a microcommunity is created and reinforced, one that has a generative potential beyond the couple of hours a month that an actual group meeting might entail. It sets a tone for and a basic mode of interaction among colleagues. As a microcommunity, it has the potential, of course, to slip into a form of cliquishness. Constructed community—especially a microcommunity of this sort—always necessitates critical thinking about that possibility of factionalism, which is as destructive a force as any other that I will mention later. Even a research support group, therefore, must have somewhat porous boundaries and welcome in regularly those who cannot or who hesitate to participate when it is first formed. While I believe that a drop-in group is not a good option, because it is too dilettantish and does nothing to establish enduring and healthy ties among colleagues, I have found that regularly (every semester or every year) reopening the membership and reissuing the invitation to join offers a balance between the exclusivity necessary for effective group functioning and the openness or porosity that mitigates against factionalism. Indeed, in both venues where I created such groups, every year that passed led to an increase in the number of members in the research group, as more and more people chose to invest in the creation of a collegial community.

But even better, and more constructive of community, is to create multiple interactive venues beyond one research group, so that macro-community members have the opportunity to choose a venue that best suits their needs and time constraints. All it takes to set up both the formal presentation brown bag that I mentioned and the writing workshop is simply to send some e-mails to colleagues, establish a calendar for scheduling, and then find a venue. Any department member or administrator can do these in an hour or two over the course of a few afternoons, and thereby act as an agent of change, a leader, in the transformation of a community.

But even those two venues should not serve as the sole occasions upon which a revitalized community should depend. It takes very little additional time to create also a reading group that focuses on a new book published in pedagogy or a methodological issue that cuts across people's individual research specializations. A reading group can draw in overlapping or perhaps substantially different groups of people who may not have new research of their own to share or who are hesitant for whatever reason about work-shopping their own writing. A reading group does not have to meet monthly; it can focus on a book that people read over the course of a semester and then meet late in a term to discuss. Even so, it offers another common nexus of interest and point of reference in an otherwise highly dispersed, and too often solipsistic, professional existence. Some campuses even sponsor monthly book discussion groups, publishing a calendar of books to be discussed at the beginning of the school year, as well as the venue for discussion, and then inviting all who wish simply to show up and participate in a discussion. This has the advantage of offering a new opportunity each month for people to decide to participate; it emphasizes those porous, welcoming boundaries that work against factionalism and regularly reinforces a dynamic of productive conversation and intellectual dynamism.

The occasions above cost nothing except for time and commitment; the same is true for topical workshops and brown bags on pedagogical issues and professional challenges, and for meetings of special-interest groups devoted to discussing specific hot topics in a group's university or departmental life. Thus, even on the cheap it is still possible to offer colleagues many opportunities to invest themselves in their community. With small amounts of funding, they can also be augmented by an active speakers series, one that brings people to campus from other institutions to broaden even further the scope of conversation on a topic or in a particular field. For just a few hundred dollars (from a department budget, dean's budget, or central funding source), a college or department can bring in someone whose perspectives will enliven hallway exchanges for days to come. Institutions, too, can become isolated and solipsistic. While that state of introversion and inertia could meet the needs of a few faculty or administrators, it is deadly. Vibrant faculty will leave or become sullen; students will encounter parochial, anachronistic perspectives. A few hundred dollars a month to bring in outside perspectives and new energy is money very well spent.

But something to remember for anyone taking on the role of agent in trying to "build" a vibrant community in this way is that no matter how many opportunities or venues you create, not everyone will avail herself or himself of one or more. Some people are simply unwilling to invest the time or energy, are for some reason already deeply invested in the status quo and have no desire to change it (even if it is, or perhaps especially because it is, highly dysfunctional), or have too many other commitments and personal responsibilities to add another one to their lives at the moment. The inevitability that some, perhaps more than a few, will choose not to participate should never discourage us from doing what we can with those who do wish to participate. If we set up a false and destructive binary of "all or nothing," then we will always end up with nothing. We have to be happy with "most" or even just "some."

But certainly those words of caution also serve as a reminder that for unprotected junior faculty members, disrupting the norms of a community (especially one that is isolated or self-satisfied in its solipsism) can carry its risks. Tenured faculty have responsibilities that go along with that award of lifetime job security. I have seen far too many newly tenured, still young, and vibrant faculty regard their award of tenure as a license to drop out. The granting of tenure is actually a license to take risks and do more ambitious and potentially disruptive work, not an excuse for withdrawing from department and communal responsibilities. From the ranks of newly tenured associate professors should come the most dynamic and interesting challenges to the preconceptions and norms of a department or institution. Granted, our lives are diverse and diversely complex, and may involve decisions on when or if we will have children and reflect the extent of our responsibilities toward aging parents and other relatives. Workaholism is not what I am extolling here. However, our lives are always enmeshed with the lives of individuals beyond those of our domestic and familial units. I am simply asking that we take all of our responsibilities seriously when we are granted the luxury of tenure; otherwise the rationale for it is seriously degraded.

But if tenured faculty in a department are particularly overcommitted or inert, and the energy driving its transformation can come only from its untenured, recently hired faculty, then I would urge anyone thinking of taking on the role of change-agent to do a cost/benefit analysis, and make decisions in self-protective fashion. As I emphasized in *The Academic Self* and reiterate in my conclusion here, we must learn to read our institutions as carefully and accurately as we would any other text or set of research data. Talk to trusted mentors, learn about past patterns of reward or punishment for similar activities, research thoroughly the institutional protections that you have if you do encounter hostility, and make a decision carefully weighing likely consequences. Part of responsibility taking is also accepting the likely outcomes of the decisions that we make. Unpleasant surprises may await any of us trying to reinvigorate a department or challenge the norms of an institution, but if we start a process knowing that we will surely create powerful enemies in the administration or among senior faculty, then we cannot be shocked when that happens. Sometimes it may be worth risking our jobs to create a better community dynamic and a context in which we can thrive intellectually. But in risking our jobs (in whatever ways that we may knowingly do so), we have to also accept the fact that we may, in fact, lose those jobs.

This also means that senior faculty, department administrators, deans, and provosts have a responsibility for speaking honestly with junior faculty about their choices and plans, and about the consequences of devoting themselves to communal work (often placed in the category of service) rather than more high-profile research, and for mentoring faculty on how best to thrive in a given institutional setting. Nothing I have said above is meant to deny the fact that some colleagues may choose inappropriately or unwisely in devoting themselves to speakers series or brown-bag lunches instead of teaching their classes responsibly or conducting the research required for tenure. That is one of the primary responsibilities of a dean or department chair: to make as transparent as possible the rules for success and how a junior faculty member is or is not succeeding in a given context. But effective communication always depends upon someone speaking precisely and effectively, and another person listening attentively and asking any necessary follow-up questions. If a junior faculty member is cautioned by a department chair about an activity and ignores or dismisses the warning, then that junior faculty member bears some responsibility for the consequences.

Because "change" always carries its risks, ideally it is part of the work of administrators themselves. It is often the department chair or dean who has the greatest ability to build a vibrant community. This can be furthered through the last venue or occasion that I will mention here, one that has a mixed reputation but still much value to it. This is the "retreat" in which a group of people meet for a full day or over a weekend in more or less continuous discussion and social interaction to perform, what I believe must be, a very well-defined task. On the university level, I have attended highly productive retreats devoted to issues such as general education/core curriculum, though including as well breakout sessions on other topics of interest. But at the college and department level, the most successful retreats I have attended have not only examined specific topics of immediate importance, but have also focused on planning for the upcoming year. This provides one more important addition to the network of occasions comprising a dynamic community, one in which common goals are articulated and an ethos of goodwill, shared purpose, and communal investment is reinforced. This can occur even in that state of disciplinary and methodological fragmentation that I mentioned earlier. In a daylong or weekend retreat, or even in a two- or three-hour college-wide or department meeting setting, we have to be able to articulate some number of shared goals (however few) in which to invest our time and intellectual energy, even if they include something as basic as increasing the number of opportunities for the mutual exchange of ideas that I just mentioned. Articulating three, five, or some other modest number of common emphases for a community for an upcoming year reminds us that even in our state of fragmentation something brings us together within a college or department, that we share a professional life even if we may not share a research agenda, pedagogy, or identity-political affiliation.

In fact, our differences are often grossly magnified simply because we fail to remind ourselves of the extraordinary overlap in view and belief that is fundamental to our choice of work in the academy. In my field of English, we do not all agree on how to teach or conduct research on poetry, fiction, or drama, but we often forget that we do commonly agree that teaching and conducting research on poetry, fiction, and drama, among other things, are worthwhile endeavors. And that sets us apart from a large percentage of the general population and gives us a communal identity that should not be blithely dismissed, forgotten, or ignored. At retreats in the past, held during particularly stressful times or in response to crises, I have used a technique that I admittedly borrowed from a pop psychological text, Richard Carlson's *Don't Sweat the Small Stuff at Work*. In an exercise he calls "Light a Candle Instead of Cursing the Darkness," he asks individuals in dysfunctional work environments to suggest positive steps toward addressing a situation instead of simply complaining about them (36–38). In my version, I asked retreat participants to preface any initial contribution to the discussion with a statement in which they mentioned something that they valued or appreciated about the department, the institution, or the careers that they have had therein. While a few sneered at the exercise, most complied, and more than a few were quite moved emotionally. It produced some of the most productive discussions I have ever had at a retreat, by shifting the dynamic from finger-pointing and complaining to one involving expressions of gratitude and humility.

These last observations bring me to a brief overview of some of the external, as well as internal, stressors that threaten the vibrancy of our academic communities. I've alluded just now to one of the external ones: a lack of respect for or understanding of what we do in the academy. This can come in various forms and threaten our well-being and even ability to teach, conduct our research, and meet the needs of our students, staff, and colleagues. Communal dialogue and planning can help us meet some of these external threats. In times of dwindling resources and funding cuts, we have to continue to speak to one another about priorities and ways of lobbying effectively for the financial support that we need to do our jobs. As I will explore in my next chapter, we are encountering a terrible shift in emphasis in the United States from the firm belief in education as a public "good" to a new definition of it as a private responsibility and financial burden. These can be depressing times for higher education, yet we do not have to sit silently and passively, allowing others to determine our fates.

Only by continuing to speak to each other can we strategize so that we can retain some measure of agency in defining ourselves and our institutional identities and not feel ourselves to be at the mercy of others who may define us in ways that we find unacceptable or demoralizing. This is an absolute necessity when we are hit with budget cuts and other threats to our financial security and integrity. If, as I have suggested, our institutions are texts of sorts that we need to learn to read critically and carefully, part of that textuality is social and political context. Retreats, brown-bag lunches, and ad hoc task force meetings can all offer venues for strategic planning on the issue of explaining more effectively to politicians and trustees our institutions' needs and work. Several insightful books are available that put into perspective the changing finances of public higher education (Duderstadt and Womack's *The Future of the Public University in America* is a fine example), ones that could jump-start a discussion. Silence breeds resentment and cynicism. Dialogue alone is no panacea; however, it is necessary, if never sufficient, for surviving and, to whatever extent possible, thriving, even in depressing times.

Often accompanying a rollback in financial support is a "speedup," to use a factory metaphor. We are expected to work harder, teach more students, serve on more committees, and even perhaps meet rising quantitative expectations for research and publication. Again, vibrancy during such times—I should say, these times—is difficult to build or maintain. However, dialogue is again absolutely necessary, if never sufficient. At the very least, and as I will discuss in my conclusion, a careful consideration of time-management skills and effective program and individual prioritization has to occur if we are to avoid being victims of a nameless, faceless "system." We should always discuss how best to respond collectively to what we do not like in our changing political and institutional environments. We can strategize about how to cut back in one area so that we can, if we have to, increase our professional activity in another, and as we talk about this we are reminded that we as individuals are not alone in being overworked or stressed. Any faculty member, with like-minded colleagues, can form an ad hoc working group on this topic—it does not have to be assigned to a group by an administrator or a program committee—and any working group can publicize its activities through e-mail distribution and through the generation of working papers or policy recommendations. As always, it is wise to understand the consequences of such actions, especially for the untenured, and it is also always possible that any recommendations or analysis will be ignored by administrators. Even so, silence is often interpreted as a passive acceptance of the perspectives of others.

Of course, the activities above take time and energy, and that proviso allows me to shift now to a discussion of a few internal behaviors and stressors that dialogue can at least mitigate. As I mentioned earlier, the refrain "I am working harder than anyone else in my department" seems to be ubiquitous across our profession. But, the fact is, most of us are working very hard, even though it is also true that we don't always know how hard our colleagues are working. Here I think administrators, especially department chairs, have a particular responsibility for publicizing the work that faculty are doing, for setting a tone of respect and understanding, and for defusing potentially volatile situations. We have to remember and remind each other that we are not each other's enemies in times of "speedup" or just busy-ness. Work does have to be delegated equitably by department chairs or deans, but colleagues also have to be reminded that most people, if never all, are working very hard in most institutional situations.

We all know a few who are not. Every institution and unit within it has its dropouts. I don't like the more popular term "deadwood" because as far as I can tell, the individuals referred to in that way often have quite a bit of vibrancy in their personal lives, but they have dropped out of many of their responsibilities to their institutions. For those dropouts who do wish to reestablish ties to their community and profession, then by all means we should work with them and continue to invite them into the communal dialogue. However, my response to those who are most committed to their dropout state is that they are there, they are unreachable unless they decide otherwise, and that if we decide to obsess about them, then we are choosing to waste our own time. Happily, they are not the norm; most of us love our work and would never "drop out." I would simply remind everyone to depend upon irredeemably "dropped-out" colleagues only to the barest extent necessary, but then simply to leave them to their own private lives and sometimes personal demons. Offer help where help is needed, but certainly let's not waste lots of conversational energy complaining about them. Complaining about them at length means not only are they not doing any work, we are also allowing them to waste our precious time and the energy that we could devote to other, more positive activities. It is, finally, the responsibility of administrators to address such situations as institutional guidelines permit.

For faculty members, a redirection of conversational energy is key to all of the strategies that I mentioned earlier in this talk. By work-shopping our research and pedagogical innovations, by giving and attending lectures, and by participating in reading groups, we are shifting our energies from talking about people or each other in gossipy, destructive ways, to talking about ideas and our future. There have been several cultural studies-based examinations of "gossip" as a strategy that allows the relatively disempowered to exercise agency in oppressive situations, and that also allows for the passing around of useful information so people can self-protect or better negotiate tricky institutional or personal contexts. I have no doubt that this does happen. But gossip more often is a misdirection of our time and conversational energy onto the idiosyncrasies of people's personal lives, sometimes exaggerated or misinterpreted, rather than the positive work that we or they are doing. Thus, my oft-repeated refrain has long been, "Talk about ideas, not about people." This is especially true when I hear others engaging in destructive criticism or faultfinding. Talk about ideas, not about people.

Finally, we are in this profession because we choose to be here. Those of us who are tenured or likely to be tenured are very lucky, even in times of budget cutbacks. Ours is still a quality of daily life and measure of job security that is rare and for which we should be profoundly grateful. If we do not love this life in the academy, if we are angry and resentful and destructive, then it is appalling that we choose to remain in the academy. It is likely our students, as well as our colleagues, are suffering; and certainly there are many others who are desperate for our jobs and who would do a superb job. Of course, the great majority of us are none of those things; we are not destructive, angry, or resentful. However, we do have to remind ourselves often that we bear responsibility, even as pretenure professors and certainly as senior professors and administrators, for building and maintaining the vibrancy that I've been discussing.

Except in the cases of the most egregious dysfunction or oppression, any one of us can be an agent for change. We also have to understand, however, that change often takes a very long time. The processes about which I have been writing here may take years before they begin to realize significant forms of success. I have known far too many faculty who start that long process of working to change their departments or institution, but then give up, because the process does not pay off dramatically after six months, a year, or two years. It may not; it may be five or more years before significant change occurs. And this is the final internal stressor that I will mention: overly optimistic expectations for change. We always have to value the incremental. Communities and institutions are inevitably conservative in that their norms and behaviors always change incrementally. Gadamer saw this, speaking often of the power of tradition that we must always acknowledge even when we resist it with all of our critical energies. That is not to apologize for institutionalized oppression nor is it to argue against trying to make change occur as quickly as possible. But it is to emphasize that we cannot abandon our projects because we are confronted with entrenched beliefs and a variety of witting and unwitting forms of resistance that slow down processes. We have to be sustained not only by the hope for grand improvements and radical changes but also by the small successes and incremental alterations that are the subunits of grand and radical change.

Have lunch with a member of your department who is not among your best friends. Set up a brown bag and don't become fatally discouraged if it is sparsely attended. Get a group of faculty together to read Jane Tompkins's *A Life in School* or Annette Kolodny's *Failing the Future*, both of which contain some provocative and very useful examples of how an individual can work to change a group of students, a department, and even an entire college. Tompkins counts among her finest professional achievements helping set up a cappuccino bar where faculty and students can chat over coffee (197). Kolodny, as a dean, worked on a larger scale to "create a sense of community and an inclusive approach to problem-solving" that involved retreats and faculty mentoring groups (179–83). Begin small conversations of your own on topics of communal interest and let those conversations spread slowly and incrementally. Investing in community means investing in it, potentially, for a very long time. If we think of our careers as ones enmeshed in community for years or even decades to come, then we are less likely to become bitter or inert if one idea fails or a series of occasions meet with disappointing results.

As I mentioned earlier, Gadamer insists that we live in unending conversation, that it is, quite simply, the human mode of being in the world. We can build on those slowly evolving dialogues to improve our institutions and our professional lives. As I will discuss at greater length in the next chapter, I even hope to see, one day, more energetic attempts to take that critical conversation well outside the physical boundaries of our institutions, to make our universities and colleges the nexuses of energetic communal conversation, rather than inwardly focused conversation alone. Only in this way can our universities become again "public goods" rather than simply private venues for an exchange of information. This would mean, of course, a significant rethinking of what a university does in the twenty-first century and what role it plays in helping educate not only its students but also its community. Whether or not that radical change is one that I will see within my lifetime, I do know that we can do a better job at talking among ourselves and nurturing those professional and intellectual energies that *are* teaching, research, and service. We as educators know that we are not wholly defined by our past and our previous ways of thinking; if we really believed that we were determined in that way, we would hardly walk into a classroom and expect that anyone would learn anything from what happens there. That same conversational vibrancy that is the best of what happens in the classroom represents also the best that can happen in an institutional context.

We are, or should be, each other's most attentive students.

chapter five

Reclaiming the University as a "Public Good"

i F THERE IS a lament common among many of the books published recently on the state of higher education in America, it is
that the "public" does not appreciate, support, and adequately reward
the hard work of the academic community. This "public" is often cast
as a homogenous mass of increasingly skeptical, even stingy, taxpayers,
who want high-quality, modestly priced education for their children, but
also impossibly low federal, state, and property tax rates. The authors of
Remaking the American University assert that "the principal responsibility
for making colleges and universities *less* places of public purpose belongs
to the public itself, or the voters and the officials they have elected to
national and state offices" (Zemsky, Wegner, and Massy, 4; my italics).
They note: "Conceived originally as institutions to serve the public well-
being through the creation of educational opportunity, higher education
institutions have become instead the thresholds delineating the advan-
taged from the rest of society" (5). Their conclusion: a "college education
is becoming a private good" (5).

James Duderstadt, the former president of the University of Michigan, echoes this, suggesting "pessimistically, one might even conclude
that America's great experiment of building world-class public universities supported primarily by tax dollars has come to an end" (Duderstadt
and Womack, *The Future of the Public University in America*, 127). David

Kirp in his book *Shakespeare, Einstein, and the Bottom Line* first cites and then expands upon Duderstadt's memorable characterization of the changes that have occurred over the past generation: "'We used to be state-*supported*,' [Duderstadt] has said, 'then state-*assisted*, and now we are state-*located*.' Some administrators, pointing to the hostility of many legislators, would go further, describing theirs as a state-*molested* university" (124–25; emphasis in original). The numbers certainly support such dire assessments: the percentage of Penn State's budget that comes from the state dropped from 54 percent in 1976–77 to 31 percent in 2001–2002, while the University of Virginia's slid from 28 percent in 1985 to around 8 percent in 2003 (Washburn, *University Inc.*, xiv). Duderstadt notes, "Between 1978 and 1998 direct state appropriations as a proportion of the total revenue of public colleges and universities declined by nearly 25 percent, despite a continued growth in college enrollments" (103). While some state appropriations have inched back up in the last year or two, in many, the numbers are at or still near historic lows, especially considering the still-increasing numbers of students being served.

The situation is certainly discouraging if you believe that public education is, in fact, a *public* good, and that public financing to ensure wide access to an education is fundamental to economic opportunity for the impoverished and to an informed, critically engaged, and intellectually vibrant citizenry. And I have other worries as well. As education is redefined as solely a private responsibility rather than a public good, that education will itself be redefined to serve the narrowest forms of self-protection and self-interest: for my $20,000, $30,000, or $40,000 a year in college costs (the sky seems to be the limit now), I want training that leads provably and immediately to a high-paying career. In fact, and as some commentators are now pointing out, I *must* have that lucrative career just to repay student loans that are roughly equal to a previous generation's home mortgage. It seems inevitable that intellectual growth, expansive knowledge seeking, and experimentation with the arts and humanities will be perceived as wastes of time and money when students are accumulating huge amounts of debt in a cost-driven rush to what must be very high-paying employment. Tamara Draut, in her compelling book *Strapped*, argues that "the debt-for-diploma system continues to exert a powerful influence on young adults even after they leave college. It influences decisions about where to live, what job to take, and even when to get married" (95). We are creating a debt-driven system of indentured servitude.

To be sure, I think there is a proper balance between cost and access that respects the limitations of public funding and taxpayer monies, and that ensures students take seriously their education by assuming some of the responsibility for paying for it. My time spent teaching in Europe has demonstrated firsthand to me that a very low-cost (still nearly free in some European nations) higher education sometimes means that students can be very irresponsible in class attendance and work habits. However, we in the United States are moving quickly to an extreme that is shocking. Draut notes that while student enrollments in college increased by 44 percent from 1977 to 2003, student indebtedness increased by 833 percent (33). She adds that in 2002, 17 percent of college graduates reported having "changed careers as a result of their student debt" (98). Jeff Williams makes the salient point that such percentages, which reflect choices after graduation, actually mask the fact that many students choose majors on the basis of perceived earning power alone, forgoing careers in education or public service because they know they cannot possibly afford such choices given their anticipated student loan payments ("New Indentured Class," B7). No one should have to mortgage their future and be forced into a set of career choices governed solely by anticipated salary levels simply to pay back the debt acquired in getting an undergraduate or graduate degree. The ethos of our entire nation is being corrupted by the abandonment of the concept of modestly priced public education as *an unequivocal public good*.

This situation demands a vibrant national conversation on the financing of higher education. As a politically active individual, I certainly demand of candidates whom I support a commitment to making that conversation a top priority. However, I also think that all of us who work in public higher education have responsibilities for initiating those conversations. Just as we cannot wait for our department chairs, our deans, or our provosts to "fix" the problems that we bemoan locally, we also cannot wait passively for local, state, or federal politicians to repair public education in the United States. We are not simply educators in the fields of the sciences, humanities, and the arts, we must also be *public* educators who are prepared to address the social roles and values of education itself. This is yet another "meta" move in the hermeneutic circle of our professional life that we must make or we will suffer ever more dire consequences for our insularity. Indeed, the numbers above and the financial situations at every public institution in this nation demonstrate that we, and most important, our students are already in a crisis that our lack of attention to the "big picture" of higher education in the United States at least abets. I am hardly saying that we in higher education are to blame for the current situation (many of us have been working very hard and at low salary levels for many years to educate the tidal waves of students who have entered our public education system), but I am saying that we are always culpable when we perceive a crisis of this magnitude, one that touches our core professional responsibilities, and then fail to address it.

Most commentators (including Duderstadt and the others mentioned above) are sure that we will never return to the days of very low-cost public education in the United States, supported primarily by generous subsidies from state and federal governments. Changing taxpayer priorities and the perceived success of alternate strategies for raising monies through corporate partnerships and donor cultivation means that our fiscal paradigms have probably shifted forever. However, here and elsewhere, we do not have to set up a false binary of "all" or "nothing"—in which "all" is a return to the previous paradigm. In that case, nothing is what we will get. Instead, it is vital that we see "some" improvement in public funding and a steady, if slow, revitalization of the link between public universities and the publics they serve as worthy and achievable goals. Our negotiations for resources and jockeying for public attention and respect will always lead to partial victories and numerous, deep compromises. That is, of course, the principle of conversation as I return to it in every chapter of this book. Explanation, understanding, and amelioration are our goals, not the resurrection of an outmoded relationship. Indeed, given the fact that there is still only sporadic conversation on the escalating costs of higher education occurring today among politicians and policy makers, simply the establishment of vibrant local and national conversations is itself one worthy goal.

And this conversation should actually involve all of us in higher education. Of course, many of my readers do not work at public institutions.

However, it is important that all faculty and administrators, including those at liberal arts colleges and private universities, participate in public conversations about the aims and affordability of higher education. No student should begin her or his working life with a crushing burden of debt. To my mind, it is shocking that even as some of our nation's most prestigious institutions gain national attention for their multibillion-dollar endowments (Harvard's is now over $30 billion) and their wildly successful fund-raising campaigns, many have done little to address obscenely high tuition and fee levels, despite their trumpeting of financial prosperity. As far as I can tell, they are concerned about students only to the extent that those students' profiles help them maintain or improve their rankings in the *US News and World Report* annual guide, which in turn, helps them improve their own fund-raising. It appears to be a vicious circle, driven by ego, *not* a hermeneutic circle demonstrating a sense of humility in a larger conversation about social responsibility and how best to serve student needs. A standout exception to this situation of social irresponsibility is the 2005 announcement by the Yale School of Music that a 100 million-dollar donation will allow them to offer tuition-free graduate education. One graduate of the school noted that students had often left that program with debts of $75,000 and with no job prospects. "How do they pay off those loans? Often that high debt forces the artists out of the profession entirely," said Joseph Pelosi, now president of the Julliard School ("Don't Stop the Music"). While Yale has addressed this problem in its graduate school of music, the entire nation is facing it across its landscape of higher education.

Certainly we in public higher education should address the situation forthrightly; indeed, doing so is a professional responsibility. To be sure, American academics who are public employees have rarely thought of themselves as government workers with attendant public responsibilities. My check may be issued by the state government, but how often do I think of the Department of Motor Vehicles drivers' test-giver as my coworker? I would argue, however, that even as "state-assisted" public employees, we do have civic, broadly civil *service,* responsibilities, most specifically those of public education and public intellectual work. And I believe that it is by assuming those responsibilities that we can work to revive our relationship with the public itself and begin to ameliorate the funding conditions that affect our students and our own work lives. We must be more proactive in serving the public beyond that tiny subset that sits in our classes.

Below I will offer some specific strategies to consider as we engage in this work, which I believe must involve a diverse array of conversations with the public. However, first I want to mention several core principles that should govern this work with the public and, especially, our attitude toward that work. There are as many missteps possible as there are potentials for success.

Public conversation must be transformative for all of the parties involved

As I discuss venues and possibilities for conversation below, I assume that we will bring to those conversations our own proeducation agendas; however, we must also bring a willingness to listen and learn. Engaging in public conversation does not mean telling people what to think, pointing out their flaws, or simply seeking affirmation for our own beliefs. It means humility and a willingness to demonstrate that we in the academy hear others' opinions, respect those opinions (even if we disagree with them), learn through our interactions, and are conscious of (and grateful for) the privileges and rewards that still characterize many careers in the academy (but only a few of those of our interlocutors from the public). We cannot ignore or arrogantly dismiss skepticism regarding tenure, long summer "vacations," and state-supported pension and other benefit plans. We have to see those inquiries as opportunities to educate without condescension.

Of course, we will still present our points of view with passion and explain with care the deep-seated nature of our beliefs and values. Humility in a conversation does not demand self-sacrifice or self-effacement. It does mean, however, that we signal that we are engaged listeners and that we are not rigid in every assertion that we make. Smugness and inflexibility will only make matters worse. However, thoughtful conversation about our research, teaching, and institutional values, imbued especially with a concern for our students, can have an impact on other participants who approach conversation with the same generosity and eagerness. Some will not; some interlocutors from the political world may be interested only in grandstanding and self-aggrandizement. But if we allow them to silence us or render us cynical, then we are responsible for that decision and its results. We will never convince all or perhaps even most participants to embrace our points of view as their own, but everyone who approaches conversation with openness and an eagerness to learn will leave it transformed. We must retain our faith that some of our interlocutors will be changed. Indeed, I would never have entered the teaching profession if I thought education of this sort was impossible or improbable.

Being multivoiced is a necessary job skill

Just as in my last chapter, where I suggested that we train graduate students to enter a profession in which they must be multivoiced, here I will remind us all of that same job skill. We already, unconsciously, adjust our voice and language to meet the needs of the situation. Most, if not all, of us speak very differently depending upon our interlocutor: a colleague across the hall, a group of freshmen, our dean, our neighbors, or our family. We do not, in fact, have a "natural" voice; instead, we have learned during our graduate training and professional lives to assume a voice or set of voices when discussing our work and when relaying information in the classroom and elsewhere. If we have always thought of our professional "academic" voice *as* natural, then we certainly need to step back and work to recognize it as constructed and malleable before assuming that we know how to speak with a nonacademic audience. Speaking to the public as we would at a conference to fellow researchers will also only worsen our situation.

Frankly, I do not think such adjustments are all that difficult to make unless we are deeply ego-invested in opaque, specialized language. As I tell students all the time when they claim that they have only one writing voice, imagine that you are explaining your ideas to siblings, parents, or others with whom you have a close, nurturing bond but who do not share your knowledge background and discourse. We should be practicing on those individuals already. In fact, one of the closest analogies to what I am suggesting here is the long-term social payoff of the "coming out" movement. For the lesbian and gay population, "coming out" in high numbers over the past thirty years has led to a dramatically enhanced awareness of queer lives and perspectives among heterosexuals in America. But for those of us who participated, "coming out" did not mean speaking with family members or the heterogeneous, heterosexual population as we would with a group of close friends at a party or a bar. It meant adjusting our language and shaping information before sharing it. Certainly, the situation today for lesbians and gays is far from perfect, but it is much better than it was a generation ago. Similarly, I believe that sharing academic perspectives and values forthrightly and carefully with family, neighbors, friends, and audiences of strangers can help break down the barriers between a skeptical public and a still-too-silent ivory tower.

Being well-informed on the state of public education in the United States should be a job requirement

Know the funding situation and the percentage changes in state support for higher education over the past ten years in your state. Know the rate of tuition increases over the same time period at your institution. Be able to explain your research, pedagogy, and service commitments in accessible language. Be able to talk about your professional values and the overall crisis in public education in the United States in careful and knowledgeable ways. This is a hermeneutic move—from the micro- to the macro- and back again—that we all must make.

I suggest that one message that we should be able to communicate effectively to the public, especially given the current political climate, is that affordable education, supported with public financing, is as important a "national security" issue as law enforcement and national defense. Our message should be clear: training in cross-cultural communication skills is a national security issue. Critical and innovative thinking about seemingly intractable national and international problems is a national security issue. Teaching the math and science skills necessary for our economy to thrive is a national security issue. Educating and providing economic opportunity to the poor and disenfranchised in our own nation is a national security issue. Public education must be a national security priority.

Public ambassadorship is always risky; tenure is indispensable

The only rationale for abandoning a tenure system is if tenure is super-fluous. If we create widgets and there is nothing controversial about widget-creation, then it is unlikely we will be fired if we continue to create widgets in meek and cost-effective ways. If tenure is designed to protect academic freedom and we do not exercise that freedom, then ten-ure is simply an anachronistic job perquisite. If we don't use it, we should probably lose it.

Of course, some of us work in identity political fields that make our research and writing risky from the start. Some of us engage in pedagogies that challenge traditional ways of teaching, some of us overturn accepted notions in our fields, and others stand up to harassment and injustice in our departments. These are some of the long-standing, and still impor-tant, rationales for tenure.

But I am adding another here in my call for all of us to engage with the public in conversations and forums that expose our research and pro-fessional values to broad scrutiny. This scrutiny will be especially intense by pundits who find our advocacy of critical thinking and tolerance of diverse viewpoints antithetical to their own beliefs and political agendas. Politicians and interest groups who are leading the revolt against taxa-tion and any public financing of education will also try to use our words and research interests against us. Tenure in a time of hyperbolic political rhetoric and vicious partisan assaults is an unquestionable job necessity if we enter that fray. We should work diligently to increase the number of tenure-line faculty in our departments, and also improve the working conditions of part-time and non-tenure-line faculty. However, the rare privilege of job security also means that the tenured among us have no excuse for letting controversial issues remain unaddressed.

• • •

With those core principles established, I want to suggest now five specific strategies for reconnecting to the public and reclaiming the university as a public good. These are not fully sufficient, but to my mind they are necessary if we are going to begin to protect our students and defend the value of publicly financed higher education.

STRATEGY ONE
Public service should be an expected and highly rewarded component of our professional lives

Many colleges and universities make some mention of "public service" in their requirements for tenure and promotion; however, it is usually embedded in a laundry list of service expectations, including work at various levels in the institution itself, and then almost invariably relegated to last-place priority. At most large universities, research is, of course, priority number one. Excellence in teaching is often mentioned as a second-place priority and will at least be rewarded modestly (or more likely punished modestly if wholly absent) in tenure, promotion, and pay raise processes. Service to the department and institution is a very distant third priority, often going unnoticed except in its complete absence. Service to the public is off almost everyone's radar.

That must change. We cannot expect to be treated as a public asset if we do not serve the public in clear and memorable ways. Yes, our teaching, when performed thoughtfully and well, is a form of service to the public that I am sure many of us congratulate ourselves on and think should be acknowledged by taxpayers and legislators. And we may be right that it should be, but it is actually hidden from the view of the public (I don't teach my classes in full view of a public audience), it is usually equated with the payment of tuition even by students ("I'm paying for this class!"), and it is certainly not designed to connect with the needs and interests of a heterogeneous audience (we have every right to use specialist language in a class when we are training would-be specialists). If our salaries are paid with subsidies from public funds and if we want that to continue, for the good of our students and the sake of our own working conditions, then we must foreground our commitment to serving the public in ways that are more than mere afterthoughts.

One possibility would be to ask every individual under review, whether pre- or posttenure, to provide a brief public service plan as part of that review and provide a few specific details about progress toward completing that plan, and specific outcomes achieved or anticipated. In that way, administrators and faculty evaluation bodies can at least assess public service responsibly and reward it appropriately, even if its effectiveness can never be measured with scientific accuracy. Certainly, its potential forms are highly diverse. Public service might include, among other things, speaking to community organizations, volunteering with social service groups, appearing in the media as an "expert," working on public boards and community oversight committees, and being involved in grassroots efforts to address community problems. The list is potentially endless, of course. However, it is vital that in all instances we make sure that our efforts serve as an opportunity for the public to see us as nonpartisan public educators whose work is connected clearly to their needs and interests. We have to be multivoiced but also on message: serving the public in visible and accessible ways is a significant part of what we do as public employees.

Indeed, we use the term "service learning" to talk about opportunities for our students to learn while working outside the classroom and the boundaries of the university. I think we also need to talk about "service teaching and learning" for the professoriate, who also must create and take advantage of opportunities to connect, learn, and teach beyond the walls of the ivory tower.

STRATEGY TWO

When discussing controversial issues, our work should be cast as genealogy, not shrill advocacy

Some of us hold very strong political beliefs, especially in the areas of identity politics, economic justice, and U.S./global relations. These may be at odds with general public opinion and the politics of the day. It is very difficult to avoid becoming combative or defensive when we hear opinions expressed that we find thoughtless, intolerant, or oppressive. But as multivoiced professionals who are also skilled teachers and supple conversationalists, we have to be able to choose the best strategy for explaining our views, while allowing others in the conversation to have their say, and with our acknowledgment of the deeply felt nature of their beliefs. Our public work, when we are representing our institutions especially, cannot be connected to partisan politics, even when it has a myriad of political implications.

Genealogy is the Foucauldian concept (derived from Nietzsche) that designates a process of uncovering both the hidden back-history and the current functioning of concepts, and exploring the power relationships that they encode and support. Foucauldian genealogy at its most memorable—of "sexuality" in the volumes of *The History of Sexuality* and the prison in *Discipline and Punish*—does not club readers over the head with a political point of view. Foucault's is a much more subtle strategy of demonstrating the timebound and therefore temporally malleable nature of most beliefs and taken-for-granted notions. He slowly leads readers to the inevitable conclusion that fixed, transhistorical "truth" does not exist, and that human beings have an active role to play in creating the conditions of justice and respect for human diversity within the context of their own day. Granted, and as I find out every time that I teach Foucault, his message of political activism in the service of greater ethical responsibility and enhanced possibilities for self-determination may be lost on some readers. But so be it. Entrenched opinions will certainly never be changed through hostile retorts and inflamed argumentation. Careful revelation of lived experiences and the opportunities for differing definitions of truth and justice are the best that we can do when conversing with heterogeneous audiences. That does not mean that we do not explain our positions with clarity and resolve, but professing them arrogantly without explanation and acknowledgment of others' views will only further entrench the perception of academics as self-centered and out of touch with mainstream America.

STRATEGY THREE

Every department, program, and institutional unit should develop at least a few public outreach goals as part of their strategic plans

Reconnecting with the public cannot be made the responsibility of individual faculty members alone; it has to be an institutional priority that administrators and the units they oversee will also be judged on in review processes. Presidents, provosts, deans, and department chairs must be evaluated on the basis of their administrative units' progress toward achieving public outreach goals. Furthermore, every unit must provide opportunities for faculty to involve themselves in public work. This could mean creating interdisciplinary panels and public forums on issues of public interest (global warming, nuclear arms proliferation, national security), or creating ongoing relationships with community groups (senior citizens associations, teachers' organizations, literacy training groups, etc.) with which faculty ambassadors work on short- and long-term projects. It might mean also creating a speakers' bureau that sends experts on various topics out into the community for accessible talks on a wide variety of issues, and hosting events that bring the public onto campus and into dialogue with knowledgeable department members (through exhibitions or creative arts events, miniseminars on specific skills such as résumé writing or public speaking, background lectures providing factual data on topics of current interest). My current department, for instance, is working to establish formal ties with a state teacher's association, helping sponsor a yearly conference to update teachers on new technology and pedagogical innovations. I also participated recently in a public forum, sponsored by another department, on the economic implications of the Hurricane Katrina debacle. These are occasions in which many nonuniversity citizens' lives are newly touched by the university.

And in all of these venues and events, it is vital to assess (through recording participation numbers or through brief evaluation instruments) the effectiveness of the work, its impact or importance, and (when possible or appropriate) the accessibility of the language used to present information. We have to be able to adjust our performances, when necessary, to make sure our message is clear: we are here to serve the public and in ways that warrant public support.

STRATEGY FOUR
Interdisciplinary institutes and centers should be evaluated on the basis of their public outreach success, and must be given the resources (and access to outlets) necessary to succeed

I am especially struck by the possibilities for public outreach by the myriad of interdisciplinary centers and institutes that have sprung up around the nation. These are entities that are already devoted to breaking down barriers and finding ways of communicating across and beyond narrow specializations. The major international organization representing such bodies, the Consortium of Humanities Centers and Institutes, now has over 150 members across the United States, Australia, Canada, the United Kingdom, Europe, and Asia. However, many of the most prestigious public institutions in this country mention no commitment to public access or service in their mission statements; that is unfortunately the case at Universities of California at Santa Cruz, Irvine, and Riverside, the University of Illinois, Rutgers University, and Penn State University. Whether or not they occasionally do offer public events, these centers have obviously failed to centralize that outreach as a stated mission. These represent missed opportunities for institutions suffering terrible declines in public financing.

I am much more impressed with the centers that do make public accessibility a key component of their mission; these include the University of South Florida, the University of Michigan, the University of Kansas, the University of Oregon, and Ohio State University. Ohio State's center is particularly impressive; not only is public outreach given prominence in its mission statement, it is demonstrated in multiple programs, including ones in which scholar/actors tour the state lecturing on and performing Ohio history, in which speakers are sent to speak at local museums on the context of visiting exhibits, in which local cultural leaders are brought to campus to lecture to university audiences, and in which the community and campus come together to discuss moral issues facing society. Most such centers focus significantly or even exclusively on supporting faculty collaboration and research, a worthy endeavor, but one that can be perceived as, and can actually be, insular and self-serving. Ohio State's, among a few others, deserves commendation for placing community needs at least on par with those of faculty.

But one of the most significant missed opportunities that I perceive is the tie-ins that are possible between the work of such centers and the media outlets often affiliated with universities. Interdisciplinary centers at public institutions should also be supported by and have their work disseminated through campus radio and television. Accessible lectures on "hot" topics, talk-show discussions on issues of local interest, skill seminars directed to meeting the needs of the broader public, and roundtables with academic and community leaders conversing on the priorities of business, of business, education, and politics are all worthy ways of reconnecting to the public. To be sure, these endeavors require modest funding and other forms of prioritization, but it would be public money well spent in the public interest and a particularly compelling goal for fund-raising campaigns. Even if the viewer numbers or radio audience is relatively small, these represent commitments and activities that can provide bullet points in publicity and advertising campaigns in which we demonstrate our public purpose.

STRATEGY FIVE

Good publicity on public service may mean financial life or death for institutions. Every unit must prioritize it

Just as colleges and departments are now, by necessity, engaging in development activities, so, too, is it necessary for them to publicize effectively their activities, achievements, and, perhaps most important, service to the public. Many units are doing "publicity" already, with a staff person dedicated to producing a yearly or quarterly newsletter, but even then, public service is only rarely a core component. Yes, faculty achievements in research and teaching should be recognized and applauded. Alumni news and events are also important to highlight since alumni provide much of the donor base that units must cultivate. But in a very real sense, the much larger base of support is the general public who must know that their tax dollars are being used in ways that add value to their lives.

I believe that this must be message number one if we wish to address and reverse the decline in public support for education. If, in fact, every unit creates a strategic plan for public outreach that it commits to and makes progress on, then every update of a Web page or issue of a publicity bulletin or alumni publication should have a significant event or achievement to report. If there is no achievement to report, then that represents a red flag pointing to a potential problem that the administrator overseeing the unit might wish to address. The efforts mentioned above can represent a multipart, coherent, and cohesive mechanism whereby individuals and units serve as ambassadors to the public and then reinforce the public awareness of and memory of that work through effective publicity campaigns. This is marketing at its most compatible with academic goals and priorities: cultivating public support for our students and our work lives that improve the conditions of student learning, as well as our teaching and research.

• • •

We have to accept, however, that any amelioration in our relationship with the public and with public funding sources can only be incrementally achieved. We cannot expect swift change and radical results or we will be disappointed and even potentially embittered. As noted earlier, Gadamer uses the phrase "fusion of horizons" to discuss the process of conversational change and the slowness of that process. In *Truth and Method* and other works, he posits our worldviews as horizons of sorts, limited by our knowledge backgrounds, affiliations, and locations. However, through the process of conversation (used metaphorically, of course, to include our encounters with books and the visual arts too) our horizons are brought into contact with those of others. When we approach conversation and those whom we encounter in it with the proper generosity of spirit and eagerness of inquiry, our horizons begin to fuse in part, leading eventually to small and sometimes large changes in perspective, but almost always very gradually and over long periods of time. The best concrete example of this I can think of is, again, the incremental results of the phenomenon of lesbians and gays "coming out" to family and friends. I know about this process firsthand. By the end of my father's life, and over a quarter century after he learned of my sexuality, his perspective had changed slowly but significantly to one of acceptance and support. That same trajectory has occurred in numerous micro- and macroways in our society, though not without many setbacks and retrenchments by those who simply refuse to engage with others thoughtfully and generously. Change is rarely quick, never linear, and almost always multidimensionally complicated to the point that it would be easy to pick out failures instead of successes if one wished to find evidence to support cynicism.

For conversation to work in this way, it is imperative that we complicate the easy (and often useful) binaries of "us/them" or "friend/enemy." The public and the politicians whom they elect are not our enemies. They have perspectives—horizons—that are very different at times from ours, but that is what makes conversation possible and even indispensable. We have to understand the financial pressures on families today that make "tax cuts" seem an uncomplicated way to boost disposable income, and we have to learn how to talk about the long-term costs of those tax cuts and the passing along of debt to the next generation. We have to understand the choices that legislators must make as they deal with constituencies demanding both lower taxes and enhanced funding for prisons, roads, and national security. We have to help them with language that translates education into a national security issue.

But also we have to get our own act together. The "us/them" binary plagues our relationships within the academy itself. Some faculty view administrators as chattering automatons, ready to "assess" and "plan" but unwilling to listen to faculty needs in the classroom and in support of research; some administrators view faculty as whiny and arrogant, unwilling to adjust their pedagogies, understand budget realities, or rise above their own petty demands. To the extent that any of those charges ring true, it is because both groups have become isolated and entrenched within their own perspectives. Internally fractured in this way, we cannot expect anyone outside of our institution to listen to us as a coherent and believable voice on the needs of higher education.

It is absolutely vital that campus conversations occur that bring faculty, staff, administrators, and students together to discuss the current crisis in funding for higher education and the values and perspectives that unite us as members of an academic community. We can agree to disagree—all conversations demand that ability—and we cannot expect to leave such conversations feeling that our individual voices were heard perfectly or accepted wholly. All of those involved in intracampus conversations must allow for the same imperfection and incrementalism in the fusion of horizons that is inherent in any conversational process. However, we have to be willing to enter such conversations assuming that common ground is preexistent and discoverable, that parties come to discussions with goodwill even if with their own standpoint epistemologies, and that we will leave conversations with our own perspectives challenged and changed. It would be disastrous to set as our sole goal to challenge and change others.

We may never agree on the best ways to spend limited amounts of money or the ideal design of curricula. Those negotiations take place every day in budget and program oversight committees. However, we can come to a better sense of a common agenda when advocating for our needs and as we attempt to reestablish strong ties to the public and our immediately surrounding communities. While certainly that process of coming to a clearer, shared message will inevitably bring to light disagreements on what fiscal responsibility means and how best to "represent" a diverse community, we have to be able to set aside intractable disagreements and focus on those common beliefs and values that we can discover. Administrators, in particular, have to be willing to allow faculty, staff, and students to have opinions and ways of being in the world that are divergent from the institution's "party line." And if faculty often seem whiny and selfish, it is largely a learned response to what they perceive as inflexibility and authoritarianism among administrators. Indeed, there is enough blame to go around for both "sides" to share in it amply.

But this makes the situation sound dire and intractable; that is far from the case in some institutions. I want to mention briefly a couple of success stories that could serve as models for us. One, I know intimately, the other only through published materials. Both demonstrate that administration and faculty coming together to prioritize ties to the community can lead to positive changes, good publicity, and a basis for further political action and future campaigns for enhanced resources. California State University, Northridge on the West Coast, and Virginia Commonwealth University on the East Coast, are exemplary in their commitment to public outreach.

When I arrived at California State University, Northridge in 1991 as a new assistant professor, this large MA-granting institution (located in the northern suburbs of Los Angeles) was desperately in need of renewal and revitalization. Its facilities were dated and visually unappealing, the campus seemed out of touch with a student population that had shifted from white middle-class to ethnically and class diverse, and its relationship with its immediate neighbors and homeowners associations was antagonistic (over parking issues, noise, and expansion). It was not a welcoming place. Its entrance and exits points were indiscernible in a maze of confusing suburban streets and sidewalks. Alumni giving and other development activities were almost nonexistent as practically no one in the San Fernando Valley saw the campus as connected to its needs or interests. It was simply a university of last resort for those local students who couldn't get into the University of California system or who needed to live at home, work, and commute to a nearby campus. The low point was the 1994 earthquake when many of us feared, not irrationally, that the very heavily damaged university was viewed as so dispensable by local residents and state officials that it would simply be shut down rather than repaired in what was then a major economic slump in the state.

That did not happen largely because a new president, Blenda Wilson, was an effective communicator, and was immediately after the quake on local news programs talking about the rebuilding of the university and staging photo opportunities with the mayor of Los Angeles and other local and national political figures. Though the earthquake occurred only a couple of weeks before the beginning of the spring semester, we reopened just two weeks late in trailers and temporary structures, and with considerable public sympathy for the losses (of life and homes and sense of well-being) among students, faculty, and staff. That horrible time of devastating loss and disruption (almost a dozen of my immediate neighbors died in a building collapse and we all lost our apartments, homes, and property) represented an opportunity for the university to change its relationship with the public and become a more integral part of the community.

Wilson and her successor, Jolene Koester, chose change and with stunningly positive results. Now promoting itself effectively as "The Intellectual, Economic, and Cultural Heart of the San Fernando Valley and Beyond," the university has been physically transformed to welcome the public onto its campus through clear signage that directs visitors into redesigned, rational streets and pedestrian thoroughfares, with thoroughly upgraded landscaping and an overhaul of physical appearance, and with a campus Master Plan that now extends to 2035. Koester, in particular, has been persistent in meeting with community leaders, speaking at local events, and publicizing the university's centrality to the identity and needs of the surrounding community. CSUN went from being an institution that was disconnected from the community and its needs to a source of pride in less than a decade. Its latest initiative is to build a performing arts center for the community. If you give back, you will, in turn, be given to. CSUN's fund-raising has leaped exponentially to nearly $20 million per year, including regular multimillion-dollar gifts and bequests, and one of $10 million, the largest cash and alumni gift to the university to date. Koester has accomplished this with unprecedented support by faculty and staff, solidified by an annual convocation address to the campus, regular coffee meetings and discussions with all members of the academic community, annual planning retreats that are very well attended, and with a personal style (as she visits faculty in their offices) that invites conversation and welcomes feedback. She is a tenured and well-published professor in the field of communication studies, and that background and skill set is evident in everything she does.

On the other side of the country, but with equally memorable results, Virginia Commonwealth University, located in Richmond, has developed a model program to connect the university to the needs of its surrounding, economically disadvantaged neighborhoods and the larger Richmond community. When he arrived in 1990, President Eugene Trani, an active scholar in U.S. history and foreign relations, saw immediate possibilities for this urban university to spearhead community development. His "Community Service Associates Program" allows faculty to take a leave of absence to work on projects in the community. This faculty/community program even predated the university's service learning program for students, which is also thriving now.

Key to these programs' successes has been the establishment of a dedicated Office of Community Programs, run out of the provost's office, with centralized responsibility for fostering community engagement. In fact, it runs fifteen different programs now, among them ones supporting student internships in local nonprofit organizations; literacy programs for local youth; a "community solutions" program that encourages local citizens to identify needs that they would like the university to address; and the "Carver-VCU Partnership" program, "a collaboration between VCU and its neighbor, the Carver community, to create a shared urban community with a commitment to improving the neighborhood's quality of life, while extending the experience of the community into the classroom and the university." But the centerpiece remains the Community Service Associates Program, through which faculty have completed numerous community projects including arts programs, literacy tutor training programs, fund-raising and administrative support programs for homeless shelters and nonprofits working with inmates and parolees, and curriculum development programs for community health workers. To my mind, this is admirable public intellectual work and cross-fertilization.

While one university in a large and diverse state system can hardly, single-handedly reverse the steep decline in governmental funding for higher education that has characterized Virginia and the nation, VCU has certainly bucked the trend of national finger-pointing at supposedly disconnected and navel-gazing institutions of higher education. President Trani was appointed chair of the Richmond Chamber of Commerce in the late 1990s, his community projects have been singled out for national praise by mayors and inner-city development organizations, and he was named "Richmonder of the Year" in 1999. All the while, he remained a publishing scholar and has even taken two sabbaticals to research and complete a book on Warren G. Harding and another study on Irish economic development. As with President Koester, he is a model academically trained university president who sees the cross-fertilization possibilities among research, teaching, service, and administration. All provide intellectual pleasures and possibilities for social transformation.

As we follow these leads and venture more enthusiastically and systematically into a broadly defined public intellectualism, obviously there are dangers to avoid. "Dare to be reductive" is one of Gerald Graff's more memorable injunctions in *Clueless in Academe,* which figured here in chapter 2. I think that is particularly good advice for those who venture into the public realm. As I discussed earlier, we have to be able to translate our ideas, our research, and our perspectives on higher education into language that will resonate with a heterogeneous audience. I would add to Graff's injunction, however, "Dare to be tactical." Know in advance what you would like to accomplish and the best ways of achieving your goals through adjustments in your performance and language. This should reflect respect for your audience and community co-workers and respect for your own agenda. We should no more enter a conversation with the public without understanding their needs than we would give a presentation to fellow academics at a conference without preparation; in both venues we should judge the background knowledge base of our conversation partners, their assumptions and likely responses to our assertions, and work with rhetorical self-awareness to make sure that our ideas and perspectives are not rejected out of hand. As a simple example, when I go home to rural Alabama and try to talk with my mother about the wisdom of accepting and perhaps even appreciating the multiethnic makeup of her children's domestic partnerships, I don't cite critical race theory, offer an annotated bibliography, or use phrases like "hybridity" and "paradigm shift." If I did, "Just shut your mouth" would be her likely, conversation-ending response. Knowing that beforehand, just as we know the likely responses of a heterogeneous public to specialized language and self-serving performances, I and we would be largely responsible for that termination.

Similarly, our strategies must look to the long term. It has taken two decades for the current public funding crisis in higher education to reach a crisis point; it may take that amount of time and more to redress the situation. We should create our own indicators of impact and incremental forms of success—an increase in audience numbers or positive evaluations of projects and events—but we cannot expect overnight miracles. Radical results take years to achieve or they are unstable and short-lived at best. When we are thinking about public outreach, we cannot articulate only one- and five-year goals; we need ten- and twenty-year strategic plans as well. Indeed, each of us has to accept the fact that we are contributing to processes that may only come to fruition after our own careers have ended. It has to be the ideal that motivates us, not the expectation of immediate gratitude and enhanced material resources. While I never expect to have children, I certainly don't hesitate to think of my work as possibly improving the lives of a next generation of students and academic employees.

In sum, our motivation and our message must consist of an appeal to the future in the context of our own consciousness of the slowness of change. That is Gadamer's reminder in *Truth and Method*. To acknowledge that entrenched opinions, what he terms "traditions," are "always part of us" (282) is to recognize that we and our interlocutors are formed discursively, and that there is no stunning break or rupture possible from our acculturation: "In fact history does not belong to us; we belong to it" (276). This state of preformation is not static: "Tradition is not simply a permanent precondition; rather, we produce it ourselves inasmuch as we understand, participate in the evolution of tradition, and hence further determine it ourselves" (293). For Gadamer, that means incremental change over time, if we are willing to engage in dialogue and acknowledge our own and others' preformations.

Our work with the public, with our peers, and with our students must be conversational, if it is to succeed. It cannot be argumentative and it cannot be pedantic. As I quoted earlier:

> To conduct a conversation means to allow oneself to be conducted by the subject matter to which the partners in the dialogue are oriented. It requires that one does not try to argue the other person down but that one really considers the weight of the other's opinion. . . . [It] consists not in trying to discover the weakness of what is said, but in bringing out its real strength. It is not the art of arguing (which can make a strong case out of a weak one) but the art of thinking. . . . (*Truth and Method*, 367)

This is the process and goal of the university as a site of public conversation that involves and exceeds the role of the university itself. It is an acknowledgment of the university as a place where students come for many reasons—vocational, intellectual, and aesthetic, and in wide varieties of combinations—but also as a venue for public intellectual exchange. Indeed, this is intellectual exchange with the public as full participants.

This process and goal has a myriad of implications for graduate student training, for undergraduate education, for faculty roles and rewards, and for administrative job descriptions. It has been a theme threaded throughout the preceding chapters of this book. It is to reimagine ourselves as participants in public life and not refugees from it. Our training of students at all levels must be with the goal of creating informed participants in public life. And if the public craves scientifically untenable explanations for natural phenomena—such as "intelligent design"—we have to engage them in a sensitive and smart conversation about that need and its science and technology-destroying effects. If the public lends credence to Machiavellian lies about supposed purges of conservatives on college campuses (when actually I and everyone else I know values deeply the diversity of our students' opinions and the conversational energy that it fosters), we must engage them in a dialogue on that topic and the misinformation that is being disseminated. Indeed, we should not simply seek to protect our own jobs and benefits, but also be active participants in the conversations that will determine the future of our profession, our nation, and our global community. If the university fails to create these conversations and participate fully in them, who do we expect will? Corporate sponsors? A profit- and scandal-driven media? It simply will not happen if we, partnering with social service and nonprofit organizations as I suggest above, do not do it.

What can you do? Start a local conversation in your department, in your university, with the community. Talk with your administrators, or if you are an administrator, with your provost. Renewing our engagement with the public is self-protective in the narrow sense of protecting and augmenting our current and future funding but also in the broader sense of protecting our society from fundamentalism and fascism. Our working assumption must be that our future is at least partially in our own hands through our ability to engage with others. To assume otherwise is simply to justify our own isolationism and egotism. We may publish a few more articles, write a book or two, get a nice raise or a comfortable promotion, but lose the world.

conclusion

. . . .

Some Reflections on
"Balance" in Academic Life

*i*N PRECEDING chapters, I discussed a truly daunting amount of work that we in the academy need to engage in. To some, it may sound like a form a frenetic workaholism that I am advocating or taking for granted here. That is not the case. Yes, we have profound responsibilities to our students, our colleagues, and the public that we must meet, but I well realize that all of us also have a myriad of other commitments, needs, and desires: physical, familial, spiritual, and recreational. None of us should so obsess about a career or set of professional responsibilities that we risk burnout, divorce, ill health, and irresponsibility in our relationships with loved ones. We must seek a life and lifestyle that balances our own diverse needs and goals, but that also reflects and respects our commitments to others: partners, children, parents, and friends.

Yet in discussing a subject as complex and as inevitably personal as "balance" in an academic life, I want to begin by exploring over the next few pages the ambiguity of the very terms that I am using, for even seemingly simple categories such as the "professional" and the "personal" are not self-evident and neatly oppositional in the academy. Indeed, the difference between what I am doing here and what some self-help gurus do daily on their talk shows involves the role of ambiguity in our lives. We cannot—or at least should not—rest comfortably on formulae when approaching highly nuanced and always dynamic situations. Ours is the much harder task of recognizing that one size does not fit all and that what is reality for you is not necessarily comfortable or even credible for me. I can only speak out of my own life and perspective in these pages, and what I offer is not meant to deny that others' lives are differently complicated and just plain different in many ways. No one voice in a conversation can or ever should claim to capture the complexities of all other points of view. My words here, from the perspective of a partnered gay man without children or caretaking duties (for the time being, at least), are offered only as an addition to a give-and-take that must involve many others whose lives I hope to hear about and learn from.

However, allowing, even embracing, that relativism does not mean a wholesale rejection of guiding principles and long-term planning. Let's not get trapped in the false binaries used often to dismiss cultural studies and other forms of inquiry informed by poststructuralism, that recognizing relativism and the partiality of any individual's knowledge base leads inevitably to chaos or, alternately, inertia. That, too, is simply not the case. Many of us writing about and living our lives in ways deeply indebted to postmodern feminist, queer, and postcolonial theory do so while working on long-term political projects that reference deeply held ideals and while also investing in enduring relationships with our partners and communities. All of these activities demand negotiation with others whose perspectives and beliefs do not fully mirror our own. But that dynamic hardly leads to stasis, but rather the opposite.

Indeed, giving up easy formulae means a lot of discussion and an energetic, conversational exchange of perspectives. As I have suggested throughout this book, we are always inside of our own standpoint epistemologies; however, we can also gain a critical distance on them by sharing our life stories, life choices, and lifestyles with others. In fact, that is the only way we have of learning about other options and different possible choices. Our lives are based on and lived in narratives; we work off of scripts, of sorts, that we inherit from others and that we synthesize and customize to make useful and appropriate for ourselves. From my perspective, there is neither a transcendental nor wholly immanent source of information about how we can or should live our lives—whether personal or professional, and whatever those two terms mean—we only have the varying possibilities that are handed down to us and that we alter in often incremental or occasionally more radical ways. While not dwelling on the autobiographical, what I can perhaps best do here is lay out some of my own definitions and decisions, to serve as one reference point in what I hope will be a broadly cast and widely engaged conversation that continues long after this book concludes.

What do I mean when I reference the concept of an "academic life"? I know, for instance, that that term is not at all analogous to what my father meant when he talked about his "work life" that somehow stood in clear contrast to his "family life," both of which also bordered and only rarely intersected with his "social life" of fellow pool players and racetrack-goers. Those neat and secure distinctions—relatively easy to make when one works as a midlevel manager for the telephone company—are ones that we in the academy sometimes use, because we have inherited the terminology, but that does not always do justice to the complexities of our daily existences. My campus life, my social life, and my home life all intersect and overlap in ways that they did not for my father in his conception of a carefully circumscribed "work life."

In fact, what an "academic life" means to me is a broadly cast "intellectual life," and it is on the basis of that personal and even idiosyncratic definition—of academic life as intellectual life—that I then try to work out what balance means to me (though perhaps in ways that my readers, too, might find useful or at least interesting). Of course, intellectualism is, itself, a loaded term, as I explored briefly in chapter 2. It is often a pejorative in American culture and popular usage, as if "thinking about things" is somehow a suspicious or perhaps simply ridiculous activity. But I want to reclaim that term as energizing, vital, and productive. It has a long, rich, and wonderfully evocative history: from the lived commitments of Simone de Beauvoir and Jean-Paul Sartre to the retheorizations of the "specific intellectual" by Michel Foucault, by way of which we in the academy might work within our immediate contexts to change our institutions, our students' perceptions of truth and justice, and our communities in the discrete ways that are at hand to us. And in defining my academic life as intellectual life, I have also come to see many of the various components of that life as potentially (even equally) vibrant fields of intellectual engagement.

My teaching, my service to the institution, and my research are all potentially vital component parts of that intellectual life as it manifests itself on campus. Thus, when I begin to think of "balance" I am not "balancing" teaching, service, and research as wholly distinct, zero-sum, or oppositionally defined subunits of something called "work," that is itself defined in stark contrast to something called a "personal life" and something else called a "social life." That would be a truly daunting physics problem. Granted, these are not all the same, but it is a fundamental, definitional choice that I make regarding my life to find intellectual importance and vibrancy in all of those arenas. I have to make decisions every day, of course, about how I will use my time, but those choices will not be determined for me by hierarchies inherited from others and adopted without interrogation and modification. Not all of us have to find all academic life activities equally attractive or fulfilling—homogeneity is not what I am calling for here, by any means—but we should at least examine critically whatever hierarchies that we have internalized and that form the basis of our choices concerning "balance."

This, then, is the first of eight general suggestions I will offer here for working toward balance in one's academic life: Define as best you can what "academic life" means to you, and how you differently value the component parts of that life. This does not have to replicate the definitions of peers and mentors and it does not have to remain static over time. In fact, this type of self-assessment of priorities and values has to take place regularly and is itself an intellectual activity, for it should involve critical reflection, interpretation, and the possibility of effecting change in our relationships, classrooms, departments, and communities. Balance always depends upon grappling first with what it is you are trying to balance and what the touchstone values are that underlie your decisions. Perfect self-transparency is obviously impossible, but clarification certainly is.

What drew you to this life in the academy? What were you seeking here and what have you found? In a sense, I stumbled into this career and any success I have had in it is a by-product of pursuing goals that were largely personal ones not tied to a single, fixed narrative of what constitutes success in the academy. Many of the professors whom I met during my undergraduate days twenty-five-plus years ago were unhappy people and certainly would not have described their lives as "balanced." They were, in their often expressed opinions, underpaid, overworked, and unappreciated—and many complained loudly about that state of affairs even to students. They were employees of a large state university, much like the ones in which I've spent my career to date. So I certainly did not enter the academy because I had some idealized image of academic life (if anything, my expectations were so modest that I have been surprised at how happy I have been). But I still eventually became an academic because I loved writing, I loved teaching, and most of all, I loved being around smart people who could talk about ideas (even if some of them did—and do—complain a lot). Those loves have sustained me during hard times and they have been ones that I often have had to remind myself of so as not to get caught up in the careerism and petty politics that can sap our good humor and undermine our sense of well-being. The complaints that I heard as an undergraduate were those of individuals who probably were underpaid and underappreciated, but who also became increasingly bitter over a sense of status deprivation in a profession where there are still stunning hierarchies of prestige and "value" (ones that too often go uninterrogated even as we critique hierarchies of gender, race, and sexual identity).

Thus, balance for me has been tied fundamentally to those touchstones of loving my writing, my teaching, and my community of smart people eager to talk about ideas. Balance for me has always also been self-articulated with a sense of skepticism regarding that careerism and career envy that I saw plaguing the lives of so many academics over the more than quarter century I've spent in and around the academy. I can write, I can teach, and I can talk about ideas with colleagues in a very wide variety of institutional contexts. This does not mean that I will be equally happy doing every conceivable job in this profession, but it does mean that I will not allow anxieties over professional prestige to draw me into a competition to succeed as measured by a set of professional standards that I do not have to accept as real for me. Those are fundamental, definitional decisions that I have made.

If we cannot to some extent determine for ourselves what will make us feel happy and fulfilled on a day-to-day basis, and if we cannot reject larger professional formulae concerning what constitutes success in a career, then we will never have any agency in working toward balance. This bears repeating because it is fundamental: you must first create your own definition of "success" in academic life. A pernicious sense of status deprivation related to an envy of other people's jobs, successes, or prestige will destroy, absolutely, any attempt to achieve balance.

But you will note so far that I haven't talked much about "academic life" in the context of what we call "personal life," and this is the second of my eight suggestions here. My own definition of how my professional life sometimes intersects with and sometimes diverges from my personal life is wholly idiosyncratic, and that will be the case for every person reading this book. What is comfortable and happiness-engendering for me will not be so for you, and vice versa . . . so please take what I say here with more than a grain, a whole shaker, of salt. My most content moments in my "life"—academic, personal, or somewhere in between—are (and these are not in hierarchical order): spent with my partner eating dinner and watching movies together, sitting in front of my computer alone and in the quiet of the morning writing, and working with colleagues on a well-defined project to improve our institution or profession. I know this about myself and to the extent possible am honest about what I need to be happy in a "life" that is subdivided only artificially and imperfectly into the "professional" and the "personal." To the extent possible I work to protect those periods of time I need—especially the two hours in the morning writing and several in the evening with my partner—as many days of the week as possible (and it is not every day) and work toward balance in that way.

All of us have to begin with some knowledge of what it is we need, and need to protect, before we can hope to achieve a balanced life. I can only make that decision for myself and in consultation with those whom I love. Where do our children, if we have them, fit into that sense of balance, our aging parents, and our friends? Attempting to articulate this does not mean overscheduling our lives—devoting fifteen minutes to petting our dogs in the morning, and then precisely thirty to chatting with our spouses. But just because we would never go to those extremes (or if we do, would find them unlivable) does not mean that we can't get a better grasp on what we need to augment and what we can reasonably cut back on in that attempt to balance our lives. Letting it work itself out without serious reflection will be as disastrous as those market economies that find their own equilibrium without checks and protections against exploitation and always increasing expectations of "productivity." Laissez-faire economics always leads to horrific oppression. A laissez-faire approach to our personal and professional relationships will lead often to anxiety, overcommitment, and even despair.

However, and this is a big however, our "lives" are lived communally and we cannot ignore the contexts in which we think of "balance." And this is the third of my eight suggestions. If we are going to attempt to prioritize or reprioritize our academic lives, we also have to understand the consequences of any changes that we make. If I decide to devote more time to my teaching and less to my writing, or cut back on committee work so I can have more time at home with my children, or cut back on my time with my children so I have more time to spend on committee work, I have to understand how that is going to impact my relationship with my children, colleagues, and students, and—on the institutional level—affect my progress toward promotion or tenure. I suggest in *The Academic Self* that we must learn to "read" our institutional environments as texts, that we acquaint ourselves thoroughly not only with their literal documents—faculty handbooks, employment contracts, tenure and promotion guidelines, etc.—but that we must also come to understand and critically engage with their unwritten norms, policies, expectations, and practices. The same is true for the many texts of our lives and relationships.

Gadamer suggests the fundamental, lived reality of this process in his concept of philosophical hermeneutics. We live in a mundane process of interpretation, of engaging with others and the world around us as we work toward understanding (even if perfect understanding is always impossible). The most important metacritical move that we must take if we are going to be responsible participants in this process is to try to understand to the best of our abilities where the other is coming from, and to accept responsibility for acquainting ourselves with the meanings and contextual motivations of the person, institution, or print text at hand. And this we have to do with institutions and administrations, as well as conversation partners and life partners and students in the classroom, if we are going to be partners rather than potential victims, or perhaps even worse, potential oppressors in those relationships. This means working to understand how others' lives are impacted by their position in a network of expectations and relationships involving gender, age, and employment status (full- or part-time, newly hired or tenured), and how limited one's own knowledge is of those different positionings. Proactively, this means researching others' needs and desires before taking definitive actions, especially when one is an administrator.

But there is also a reactive component to this dynamic. On far too many occasions, I have heard faculty complain about some action or evaluation made by a department chair, a committee, or a dean, but when

I ask them that very question, "Tell me to the best of your ability where that other person (or group) 'is coming from'"—in other words, the presuppositions, values, perspectives that underlie the accursed action—the self-described "victim" cannot answer the question other than in an expression of outrage or angry rejection of even the need to understand that other's positioning or viewpoint. Even in a case of a duplicitous or unfair use of power, or other act of injustice, that response ("I don't know and I don't want to know") is a dead end; it leads to no possibility of effective response. It certainly does not do justice to an "academic life" that in any way purports to be an intellectual life. If, moreover, we do not pursue that knowledge beforehand—how will my institution and the actors within it respond to my activities and reprioritizations?—we will inevitably be surprised, and perhaps unpleasantly so, when it is their turn to respond in the conversational process that is academic life.

Only by knowing what balance means to us, and then what expectations our institution and colleagues have of us, can we begin to plan carefully and self-protectively about what changes we would like to make in our "academic lives." This leads to the fourth of my eight suggestions: take stock of what you want to accomplish and choose discrete goals carefully. Part of the reason that many lives can be termed "out of balance" is because we simply take on too much, unwittingly and even haphazardly. I suggest in *The Academic Self* that we all write and regularly return to a sort of personal "mission statement," that we put into writing so we can better remember the priorities and primary goals that we have for the next year, two years, even five years. This can work as a preventative (so we know how to evaluate new opportunities that arise that might overload us or render our cherished projects impossible to complete) and it also works as a necessary step in any reprioritization, which again demands that we isolate among a myriad of possible activities and interests a more select few that will receive our attention. This is a principle of what we might call career and academic life "management" as much as it is a response to a career or life in crisis.

I regularly say "no" to tempting additions to an already busy academic life. Indeed, we all have to remind ourselves that sometimes we have to say "no." For women in the academy and for members of underrepresented groups who are besieged by requests for service, the situation can be especially difficult and dire, and administrators have an undeniable responsibility to become aware of and help redress inequities. But self-protection and the protection of one's own personal life and career, within boundaries of continuing professional responsibility, are also of paramount importance, over and beyond what a department chair or dean might do. In offering this suggestion, I don't mean simply finding a way to decline to serve on a tenth committee in our colleges or departments, though that is certainly something we may need to learn to do (unless we want to serve on ten committees), but also saying "no" to opportunities that seem very appealing at first glance but that will probably distract us from other, more important, goals, because they require time. We might have to say "no" to possible conference presentations, to inquiries about writing essays or reviews, or to requests to serve on various boards and panels, all of which might be possible for us occasionally, but which can also keep us from working on the book that we desperately want to write or preparing thoroughly for the class that we are teaching or completing work on the curricular revision that we see as our most important task at the moment. Know and remind yourself often of your priorities. Write a brief narrative that you keep on your desk, or make a list and post it on the wall of your home office, whatever will remind you of those priorities. Revise it when necessary. But don't lapse into an easy, at times even chosen, forgetfulness or well-intentioned rush to accumulate new, exciting projects when the old ones aren't even completed.

Number five on my list of suggestions for balancing one's life follows from the above: work with "time" as best you can. This seems so simple and obvious as to be almost laughable, but I am still stunned at how loosely and haphazardly—sometimes even irresponsibly—many people in the academy engage with one of the fundamental dimensions of our existence: temporality. Again this is not a call to live a Fordist nightmare of excessive calculations and time-and-motion studies. Indeed, there is a huge swath of gray area between the extremes of a wholly intuitive, impressionistic temporal existence and an obsessive/compulsive approach to "time management." Let us live in that gray area more decisively.

I've mentioned some of my own "tactics" in *The Academic Self*; I'll repeat a few and add a couple here. A simple one: most of us keep day planners and/or palm-pilot-like organizers, but—I know from experience—these can be of various use values depending upon their fundamental design. Yes, it is helpful to see "at a glance" what appointments are scheduled for the day, as we do in one of those hour-by-hour planners or displays ("day at a glance"). But focusing solely on "the day" as the basic unit of time consciousness delimits my academic life—specifically, its deadlines and my responsibilities in meeting them—far too narrowly for my purposes. If I look at my day planner in the morning and focus intensely on the next eight or ten hours to come, I will no doubt be responsible in meeting my most immediate obligations. But unless I have annotated that planner with the microdetails of what I need to do today to meet deadlines coming up next week and next month, I am (to use a cliché) seeing only the closest trees and not the forest. There is an obvious comfort in knowing that we can see and fulfill our responsibilities vis-à-vis our work day. But our academic lives—our teaching, writing, and service activities—only rarely involve eight- to ten-hour projects. I also need to remember today what I've committed to finish a month or even a year from now.

This may sound trivial but it is not, because it concerns how we conceptualize our "academic lives." If we do not get the books written that we desperately desire to write, the curricular redesign projects accomplished that we feel are necessary for the vitality of our institutions, the reading groups established that I discussed earlier as one way of invigorating our departments or colleges, or even just the batch of papers graded that we promised to return to our students, it is often because we attend only to what is most immediately at hand—the person at our office door or the two o'clock meeting with the honors committee—but forget to find time for the chapter we are supposed to be writing or for the paperwork we need to complete on the project that we have prioritized. So—and these are a few practical, personal choices that I make—I don't use the "day" as my basic unit for planning. I always use a "week at a glance" style appointment book/organizer, so that every morning I see the week's obligations. I also keep a very large monthly calendar hanging beside my work station at home, with major commitments noted on it. Finally, I use a white (dry erase) board with longer-term goals and deadlines written out that I need to remember, also placed near my work station. To continue with the metaphor above, I have learned the hard way that focusing solely on "the day" means that the forest may be on fire while I am looking obsessively at the tree in front of me.

That multilayered attention to "time" allows certain protections on my part. I don't want to forget deadlines so that I have to work far into the night writing a conference paper immediately before presenting it. Nor do I want to have to work into the evening several days in a row to try to write a report due to a committee or the dean's office. I do not want to engage in those "academic life" activities after 5 P.M. I want to spend time with my family and my friends, perhaps reading or attending a community function, but not writing or grading papers. Others will want to organize their evenings differently and have their mornings and late afternoons free for their children (I know well from friends' experiences that sometimes after the kids are off to school and later when they are in bed is the only free time even available for "organizing"), but you can only set boundaries that will mean anything if you do not forget what you have to try to accomplish today so as not to miss a deadline looming next week or next month.

My sixth suggestion: subdivide your tasks and goals, and appreciate the "incremental." I discuss this in *The Academic Self,* but I think it is worth elaborating upon here. Every professional task that we take on and every goal that we set for ourselves involves a process that will lead to its completion or its failure. Teaching involves the process of class preparation and grading; research involves the various steps that lead up to its dissemination; and service—whether program management or curricular redesign—involves meetings, proposal or document generation, and a variety of other mundane activities. I would never suggest that we can exercise "control" over these; there are too many surprises, interruptions, and redirections in our daily lives to allow anything like "control." However, we certainly can attend closely to the component parts of almost any professional activity to better balance our lives vis-à-vis that activity.

I have used a very mundane example before. After many years of sitting in front of computer screens and struggling with a dissertation and the writing of several books to date, I know that I can produce about one to two pages of new writing per hour—sometimes a little less, occasionally a little more. If I spend even just an hour or so per day writing, working at least to the point where I have written a page or two, and I do so almost every day, Monday through Friday, I can produce a rough draft of a book within one year. Write one to two pages a day and you will have a book-length rough draft in a year. Of course, it may take me two more years to revise that very rough draft, but at least I have something on the page. The same incremental process holds true for any large project that we take on: program creation, the redesign of a major or minor, or grading a batch of papers. If we focus on the enormity of the project and the final outcome only, we can be paralyzed. If we break it down into some of its smallest subunits and build some attention to those increments into our daily or weekly lives, we can avoid paralysis and the catastrophic consequences of procrastination. Focus on the daily or weekly increments that you need to attend to and that will add up to the larger product or outcome that you desire.

This attentiveness does not mean an attempt to exercise control. In fact, I want to make an even broader statement here about how we conceive of ourselves in the academy. My seventh recommendation: give up the concept of "mastery" as our touchstone for academic identity. We need to reconceive our academic selves as ones demonstrating continuous intellectual engagement, but not depending upon the goal of or a state of mastery. I have mastered nothing in my academic life, not a particular subject matter, not an administrative skill set, not a pedagogy, and certainly not academic "life" itself. Everyone reading this book will, of course, have life circumstances and professional complexities that I cannot even imagine and about which it would be the height of arrogance for me to assume I have masterful knowledge. Indeed, if we think we have mastered something or that we have to master in order to be successful academics, we are lying to ourselves and setting ourselves up for easy derailment or bitterness. Mastery, finally, is a concept born of egotism and insecurity. We have to be content with continuous intellectual engagement and the joys that such engagement offers. And we must seek fulfillment in the ways that such engagements are enacted on a daily, incremental basis. That redefinition, away from mastery and toward continuous engagement, is one useful step toward achieving "balance" in our academic lives.

This focus on the incremental leads me to my final suggestion: remind yourself often that change usually occurs very slowly. Rebalancing your life will not happen overnight. Changing your department or college will not happen overnight. I have seen too many worthwhile academic, as well as broad social, projects fail because participants expected quick results. To reference Gadamer again, we are always bound by our traditions—personal, institutional, and variously social—that alter very, very slowly. We are all creatures of habit, otherwise we could not exist in the complexity of a single day's requirements for decision making. We live in language and the discursive norms through which we are acculturated as subjects in our careers and social lives. In the rush of modern communication, transportation, and technology, we can easily forget that we and those around us actually change very slowly. If we set incremental goals for ourselves, appreciate the small steps, and remain patient and forgiving, I believe we can all avoid burnout, bitterness, and cynicism in our academic lives.

• • •

There is an intriguing social movement that has garnered attention recently and that has something to say about this topic of lives in and out of balance. The "Take Back Your Time" movement is devoted to addressing the terrible *im*balances created by increasing workloads today. Its main spokesperson is the documentary filmmaker John de Graaf, but the movement also has academic ties in its nonprofit sponsor, the Center for Religion, Ethics, and Social Policy at Cornell University. A couple of the movement's basic tenets are pertinent to my discussion here. Jerome Segal in an essay in de Graaf's collection, *Take Back Your Time*, says that for those individuals who are overworked, overburdened, and at risk of burnout, there are three ways of taking back time: "1) Sell less of it: work less at those things you get paid for. 2) Prevent other people (or circumstances) from extracting it: end those situations in which, against your will, you are forced to devote your time to things you would rather not do. 3) Use your time (at work or at home) in ways that make it truly and deeply your own" (211).

As academics, especially those of us with the privilege of tenure and full-time employment, we probably cannot "sell" less of our time unless we go on phased retirement or convert to part-time status, which would mean giving up many of the benefits—material and communal—that may have drawn us to this profession. But we can certainly reflect on how we can prevent people and situations from squandering our time (what Segal calls "time thievery") and how we can use our time more meaningfully (ending what he terms "time estrangement"). As an example, what makes service so odious for some people in this profession is the perception that it is a "waste" of time—with inefficiently run meetings, fuzzy agendas, and a feeling that one is simply participating in a bureaucratic fad. Certainly assessment and strategic planning processes can often elicit cynicism for the very reason that they seem to require inordinate amounts of time that are being commandeered simply to fill up report documents destined for a file cabinet. Of course we feel estranged from our time and work if, in Sisyphean fashion, we believe we are rolling out a report that exists only to precede the next report we have to roll out.

But that is an attitude toward, rather than a fact of, our existence. Yes, our time can be wasted, but it doesn't have to be. If we are individually very good at running efficient meetings we should be volunteering to chair committees rather than simply complaining about how others chair committees. It often takes far less time to run meetings ourselves if we run them well rather than letting others do the "work" but do it poorly.

Many aspects of our work from which we might feel "estranged" are only so because we haven't defined our goals in productive and useful ways. When I speak to colleagues about strategic planning or assessment, I always emphasize that whether or not we are being enjoined to do something that is faddish or destined for the back of a file cabinet in someone's office, we can always make the task our own, and glean from it information that we can use locally in ways that may or may not have been intended by the originators of the mandate. We can make communal vibrancy one of our strategic goals; we can assess the effectiveness of our pedagogies in ways that lead to dynamic discussions of how we have or have not created effective learning environments. If we are estranged from our work, *we* need to self-assess, because often the estrangement results from our attitudes about our work, not the work itself. Yes, there are oppressive and intolerable job situations that some of us find ourselves in. But for those of us who are fully employed with tenure, and who are reasonably compensated, our "work" lives are unparalleled in how they offer us meaningful ways to live our lives, interact with others, and bring about social change.

Indeed, that concept of "time thievery" should never be used to excuse our own selfish actions or problematic attitudes. Two real-life examples: one is an academic acquaintance who, because he defined himself as a "writer" (who used his academic job simply to pay his bills) and wished to maximize the amount of time that he could devote to writing, said once, "Frankly, if I can get you to do some of the committee work that I don't want to be bothered with, that just shows how smart I am and how stupid you are." That attitude—starkly revealed there but underlying a lot of uncollegial behavior that I've seen over the years—demonstrates the pernicious effects of defining our "academic life" without reference to the community of our departments and institutions. Incidentally, that same colleague later lost his tenure-track job for abusive behavior that reflected his basic philosophy.

The other example is a colleague who, when offered the opportunity to join a research-sharing group of the type I discussed in a previous chapter, rolled her eyes and said, "Ugh, can't do it, I'm on too many other boring committees already." If interacting with one's colleagues about their most exciting ideas and sharing with them one's own intellectual passions is considered "boring committee work," that also reveals a potentially problematic vision of an academic life. I highlight these two examples to point out simply that complaints about imbalance may have roots in any number of individual conceptions about what an ideal academic life "would be"—in both cases just mentioned, a life without having to interact with colleagues at all—that may not be ones that would stand up to a test of being communally responsible. Our academic life is a life shared with others in the academy, with our families and partners, and within a much larger sociocultural and political context. Selfishness and solipsism are plagues threatening all aspects of those lives.

A final piece of useful commentary that is offered in the *Take Back Your Time* collection is expressed by a career counselor: "Planning one's life and taking actions without a conscious vision of a desired future is like driving a car while looking in the rear view mirror" (quoted in Myers et al., 155). If any one of us feels that our academic life is "out of balance," we have to take responsibility for defining for ourselves precisely what type of life we would like and how our current life needs to change. It is to consciously revisit our "life plan," as Paul Ricoeur suggests. However, and as I noted before, the changes resulting from any such revisiting and revisioning can only be done responsibly with careful reference to the lives and needs of other members of our academic and domestic community, and with a careful assessment of our own presuppositions about our "work" and what constitutes "success" in and around it.

There may be many barriers to realizing the vision of the academic life that you wish to lead, to achieving the balance that you find personally desirable, but you certainly can claim your own agency in defining that vision and balance, and strategizing in the ways that I have mentioned and in many others that will occur to you individually and collectively to achieve a better balance. Articulate to yourself, your colleagues, and your significant others that "conscious vision of a desired future." There is no one vision that all of us will share. What is workaholism to one person will be a vibrant, exciting life to another. What is an untenable daily routine from my perspective will be a nuanced and careful juggling of responsibilities for someone else. For some of us, family life provides a source of deep satisfaction that is unparalleled by any aspect of our work. For others of us, passionate about what we are writing, sitting in front of a computer screen working late on a Tuesday night or early on a Saturday morning will be as exhilarating as sitting in front of an easel was for Georgia O'Keeffe. Those are idiosyncratic, internal states of being and valuation, not ones that should be determined by others' success stories or any expectation of fame or applause. Nevertheless, none of us works or lives alone, and our decisions about balance must be made communally, for only in hearing about your needs can I better assess the communal impact of my demands. And only in learning about how my hours in front of the computer screen impact the life and needs of my partner can I seek a balance that is not simply self-serving.

The key here, as it has been throughout this book, is dialogue. If we do not talk to each other, often and at length, about our differing perspectives and insights, our loves, needs, and priorities, we may lead a life that is "academic" in the pejorative sense of trivial or of questionable importance, but not one that fulfills the very highest potential of the "academic," which is nothing less than personal, institutional, and broad communal transformation.

works cited

. . . .

"Academicself Blog." http://academicself.blogspot.com

Booth, Wayne C. *The Rhetoric of Rhetoric: The Quest for Effective Communication*. Malden, MA: Blackwell Publishing, 2004.

Carlson, Richard. *Don't Sweat the Small Stuff at Work*. New York: Hyperion, 1998.

"Carver-VCU Partnership." Online at http://www.vcu.edu/ocp/programs/carvervcu/.

Code, Lorraine, ed. *Feminist Interpretations of Hans-Georg Gadamer*. University Park, PA: Pennsylvania State University Press, 2003.

___. "Introduction: Why Feminists Do Not Read Gadamer." In Code, *Feminist Interpretations of Hans-Georg Gadamer*, 1–36.

Damrosch, David. *We Scholars: Changing the Culture of the University*. Cambridge, MA: Harvard University Press, 1995.

Davis, Angela. *An Autobiography*. New York: International Publishers, 1988.

___. "Reflections on Race, Class and Gender in the USA." In James, *The Angela Y. Davis Reader*, 307–25.

de Graaf, John, ed. *Take Back Your Time: Fighting Overwork and Time Poverty in America*. San Francisco: Berrett-Koehler Publishers, 2003.

"Don't Stop the Music: Yale Makes Music Grad School Free." CNN.com. Online at http://www.cnn.com/2005/EDUCATION/11/07/yale.freemusic.ap/index/html. Accessed November 8, 2005.

Draut, Tamara. *Strapped: Why America's 20- and 30-Somethings Can't Get Ahead*. New York: Doubleday, 2005.

Duderstadt, James J., and Farris W. Womack. *The Future of the Public University in America: Beyond the Crossroads*. Baltimore and London: Johns Hopkins University Press, 2003.

145

Eliot, George. *Daniel Deronda*. 1876. Reprint. London: Penguin, 1986.

___. *Middlemarch*. 1872. Reprint. New York: Signet, 1981.

Faubion, James D., ed. *Power: Essential Writings of Foucault 1954–1984*. Vol. 3. Translated by Robert Hurley and others. New York: New Press, 2000.

Foucault, Michel. *Discipline and Punish: The Birth of the Prison*. Translated by Alan Sheridan. New York: Vintage Books, 1995.

___. *The History of Sexuality: Volume 1*. Translated by Robert Hurley. New York: Vintage Books, 1978.

___. "So Is It Important to Think?" In Faubion, *Power*, 454–61. .

___. "Truth and Power." In Faubion, *Power*, 111–33.

Fuss, Diana, ed. *Inside/Out: Lesbian Theories, Gay Theories*. New York and London: Routledge, 1991.

___. "Inside/Out." Introduction. Fuss, *Inside/Out*, 1–10.

Gadamer, Hans-Georg. "Destruktion and Deconstruction." Translated by Geoff Waite and Richard Palmer. In *Dialogue and Deconstruction: The Gadamer-Derrida Encounter*, edited by Diane P. Michelfelder and Richard E. Palmer, 102–13. Albany: State University of New York Press, 1989.

___. *Gadamer in Conversation: Reflections and Commentary*. Edited and translated by Richard E. Palmer. New Haven and London: Yale University Press, 2001.

___. *Philosophical Apprenticeships*. Translated by Robert R. Sullivan. Cambridge, MA: MIT Press, 1985.

___. *Truth and Method*. 2nd rev. ed. Translated by Joel Weinsheimer and Donald G. Marshall. New York: Continuum, 2003.

Graff, Gerald. *Clueless in Academe: How Schooling Obscures the Life of the Mind*. New Haven and London: Yale University Press, 2003.

Graff, Gerald, and Cathy Birkenstein. *They Say/I Say: The Moves That Matter in Academic Writing*. New York and London: Norton, 2006.

Grondin, Jean. *The Philosophy of Gadamer*. Translated by Kathryn Plant. Montreal: McGill-Queen's University Press, 2003.

Hall, Donald E. *The Academic Self: An Owner's Manual*. Columbus: The Ohio State University Press, 2002.

___. *Fixing Patriarchy: Feminism and Mid-Victorian Male Novelists*. New York: New York University Press, 1996.

___. *Queer Theories*. Basingstoke and New York: Palgrave Macmillan, 2003.

___. *Subjectivity*. New York and London: Routledge, 2004.

___, ed. *Professions: Conversations on the Future of Literary and Cultural Studies*. Urbana: University of Illinois Press, 2001.

Hall, Donald E., and Susan S. Lanser. "That Was Then, This Is Now, But What Will Be? A Dialogue between Two Generations of Professors." In Hall, *Professions*, 202–23.

Harpham, Geoffrey Galt. "The End of Theory, the Rise of the Profession: A Rant in Search of Responses." In Hall, *Professions*, 186–201.

Hekman, Susan. "The Ontology of Change: Gadamer and Feminism." In Code, *Feminist Interpretations of Hans-Georg Gadamer*, 181–202.

Hoffman, Susan-Judith. "Gadamer's Philosophical Hermeneutics and Feminist Projects." In Code, *Feminist Interpretations of Hans-Georg Gadamer*, 81–107.

Hofstadter, Richard. *Anti-Intellectualism in American Life*. New York: Vintage, 1962.

hooks, bell. *Teaching to Transgress: Education as the Practice of Freedom*. New York and London: Routledge, 1994.

James, Joy. *The Angela Y. Davis Reader*. Oxford: Blackwell, 1998.

___. "Introduction." James, *The Angela Y. Davis Reader*, 1–25.

Kennedy, John F. *Profiles in Courage*. 1956. Reprint. New York: Perennial Classics, 2004.

Kirp, David L. *Shakespeare, Einstein, and the Bottom Line: The Marketing of Higher Education*. Cambridge, MA: Harvard University Press, 2003.

Kögler, Hans Herbert. *The Power of Dialogue: Critical Hermeneutics after Gadamer and Foucault*. Translated by Paul Hendrickson. Cambridge, MA: MIT Press, 1999.

Kolodny, Annette. *Failing the Future: A Dean Looks at Higher Education in the Twenty-first Century*. Durham, NC: Duke University Press, 1998.

McLaughlin, Thomas. *Street Smarts and Critical Theory: Listening to the Vernacular*. Madison: University of Wisconsin Press, 1996.

Miller, J. Hillis. "Vital Diversity: An Interview with J. Hillis Miller." In Hall, *Professions*, 224–35.

Myers, Irene, Larry Griffin, and Barbara Schramm. "A New Bottom Line." In de Graaf, *Take Back Your Time*, 154–59.

Nehamas, Alexander. *Nietzsche: Life as Literature*. Cambridge, MA: Harvard University Press, 1985.

Nietzsche, Friedrich. *The Gay Science*. 1882. Translated by Walter Kaufmann. Reprint. New York: Vintage, 1974.

——. *Unfashionable Observations*. 1873–75. *The Complete Works of Friedrich Nietzsche*. Vol. 2. Translated by Richard T. Gray. Stanford, CA: Stanford University Press, 1995.

Readings, Bill. *The University in Ruins*. Cambridge, MA: Harvard University Press, 1996.

Reagan, Charles E. *Paul Ricoeur: His Life and His Work*. Chicago: University of Chicago Press, 1996.

Rhodes, Frank H. T. *The Creation of the Future: The Role of the American University*. Ithaca, NY, and London: Cornell University Press, 2001.

Ricoeur, Paul. "The Conflict of Interpretations: Debate with Hans-Georg Gadamer." In *A Ricoeur Reader: Reflection and Imagination*, edited by Mario J. Valdés, 216–41. Toronto: University of Toronto Press, 1991.

——. "Intellectual Autobiography of Paul Ricoeur." In *The Philosophy of Paul Ricoeur*, edited by Lewis Edwin Hahn, 1–53. Library of Living Philosophers. Vol. 22. Chicago: Open Court, 1995.

——. "Life: A Story in Search of a Narrator." In Valdés, *A Ricoeur Reader*, 425–37.

——. "On Interpretation." In Paul Ricoeur, *From Text to Action: Essays in Hermeneutics, II*, 1–20. Translated by Kathleen Blamey and John B. Thompson. Evanston, IL: Northwestern University Press, 1991.

——. *Oneself as Another*. Translated by Kathleen Blamey. Chicago and London: University of Chicago Press, 1992.

——. "The Tasks of the Political Educator." In Paul Ricoeur, *Political and Social Essays*, edited by David Stewart and Joseph Bien, 271–93. Athens: Ohio University Press, 1974.

Segal, Jerome. "A Policy Agenda for Taking Back Time." In de Graaf, *Take Back Your Time*, 211–18.

Simms, Karl. *Paul Ricoeur*. New York and London: Routledge, 2003.

Spinks, Lee. *Friedrich Nietzsche*. New York and London: Routledge, 2003.

Tiruncula. Blog posting. June 6, 2005. http://academicself.blogspot.com/2005—06—01—academicself—archive.html.

Tompkins, Jane. *A Life in School: What the Teacher Learned*. Reading, MA: Addison-Wesley, 1996.

Valdés, Mario J., ed. *A Ricoeur Reader: Reflection and Imagination*. Toronto: University of Toronto Press, 1991.

Vasterling, Veronica. "Postmodern Hermeneutics? Toward a Critical Hermeneutics." In Code, *Feminist Interpretations of Hans-Georg Gadamer*, 149–80.

Warnke, Georgia. "Hermeneutics and Constructed Identities." In Code, *Feminist Interpretations of Hans-Georg Gadamer*, 57–80.

Washburn, Jennifer. *University Inc.: The Corporate Corruption of American Higher Education*. New York: Basic Books: 2005.

Williams, Jeffrey. "A New Indentured Class." *Chronicle Review* 52, no. 43 (June 30, 2006): B6–7.

Wright, Kathleen Roberts. "(En)gendering Dialogue Between Gadamer's Hermeneutics and Feminist Thought." In Code, *Feminist Interpretations of Hans-Georg Gadamer*, 39–55.

Zemsky, Robert, Gregory R. Wegner, and William F. Massy. *Remaking the American University: Market-Smart and Mission-Centered*. New Brunswick, NJ: Rutgers University Press, 2005.

index

· · · · · · · · · · · · ·